50 STATES

STATE SHAPES

50 STATES

A State-by-State Tour of the USA

ERIN McHUGH

Illustrated By
ALFRED SCHRIER

★

Additional Illustrations By
JEFF SUNTALA

BLACK DOG
& LEVENTHAL
PUBLISHERS
NEW YORK

Library of Congress Cataloging-in-Publication Data available upon request.

Published by Black Dog & Leventhal Publishers, Inc.
151 West 19th Street, New York, NY 10011

Distributed by Workman Publishing Company
225 Varick Street, New York, NY 10014

Design by Sheila Hart Design, Inc.
Printed in China
ISBN: 978-1-57912-851-7

h g f e d c b a

CONTENTS

INTRODUCTION

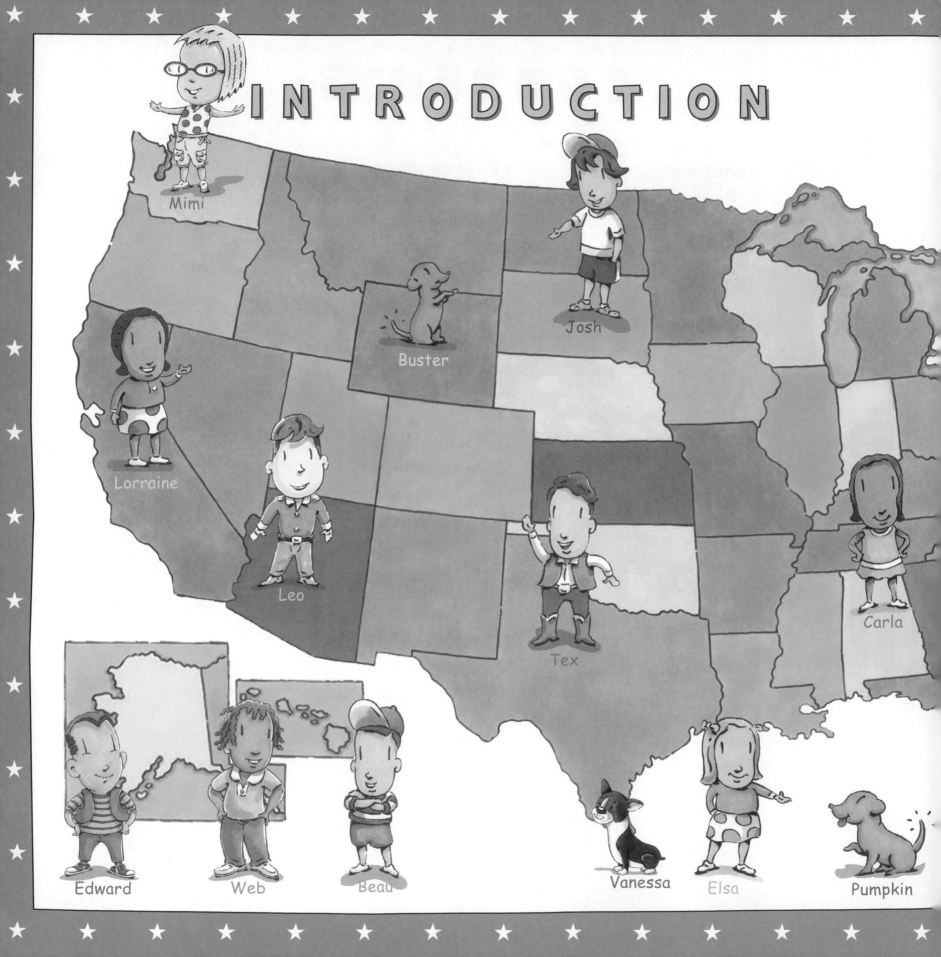

Mimi

Josh

Buster

Lorraine

Leo

Tex

Carla

Edward

Web

Beau

Vanessa

Elsa

Pumpkin

Good afternoon, everyone, and welcome to Washington, D.C.'s National Museum of American History. I've heard you kids are from all over the United States, but I know one thing you have in common—our American flag! Let's head over to my favorite exhibit—it's called "The Star-Spangled Banner: The Flag that Inspired the National Anthem." Who knows when our Stars and Stripes were first flown?

I do! Over Fort McHenry in my home state, Maryland. When Francis Scott Key saw the flag, it inspired him to write our national anthem, "The Star-Spangled Banner."

That's right, Josh. Now, I know you all are here because you won an essay contest, writing about your home state.

Well, not necessarily. I just met Leo, who's from Arizona, and he wrote about the Grand Canyon. But I'm from New Jersey, and I wrote about the sculptor who made Mount Rushmore in South Dakota.

I'm from New Bedford, Massachusetts, and I wrote about whaling, and about scrimshaw, which is this kind of art sailors used to make from carving and drawing on whales' teeth.

I studied the Amish!

Volcanoes!

I won the contest in Illinois, *plus* I can nibble a saltine into the shape of Florida.

No way!

Becky

Bernie

Scooter

Peter

Kevin

Rick

Teddy

Chris

Meredith

Julie

Skipper

J.P.

Teddy   Lily   Anita   Penny   Rufus   Sessalee   Madeline   Scott

Sounds like you all know a lot about how America was formed—from the thirteen original colonies to the Louisiana Purchase, the Civil War right through Manifest Destiny out west.

We learned all that in school. But in our essays, we got to write about all kinds of cool things. History, geography, famous people, inventions—how our country came to be is awesome. Sometimes you just have to do a little detective work . . .

For example: everyone knows about the Pilgrims, but did you know about Jamestown, which was settled in Virginia years before, or the settlement in North Carolina that mysteriously disappeared altogether?

Yeah, like you learn about Lewis and Clark in class, but how much do you know about Sacagawea, the woman who traveled with them? They probably couldn't have made it without her.

Did you know Thomas Edison was in the movie business before Hollywood even existed?

Or that you can visit a house made entirely of coal?

And the Underground Railroad—which isn't even a railroad!

See what I mean? Hey, I know what—how about we all tell one another what we found out about our country?

Moe   George

Carrie   Laura   Barney   Maggie

A L A B A M A

Alabama was the 22nd state in the USA; it became a state on **December 14, 1819.** For a long time, Alabama's economy relied on cotton plantations, and because of that, slave labor.

State Capital:	Montgomery
State Bird:	Yellowhammer
State Game Bird:	Wild Turkey
State Flower:	Camellia
State Wildflower:	Oak-Leaf Hydrangea
State Tree:	Southern Longleaf Pine
State Tree Fruit:	Peach
State Fruit:	Blackberry
State Horse Show:	The Alabama Championship Horse Show
State Horseshoe Tournament:	Stockton Fall Horseshoe Tournament
State Mammal:	Black Bear
State Horse:	Racking Horse
State Nut:	Pecan
State Quilt:	Pine Burr Quilt
State Shell:	Johnstone's Junonia
State Spirit:	Conecuh Ridge Alabama Fine Whiskey
State Nickname:	Heart of Dixie, Yellowhammer State
State Motto:	"Audemus jura nostra defendere" ("We Dare Defend Our Rights")

Q. What is Henry Louis Aaron of Mobile famous for?

Josh, this town has a weird name.

With lots of awesome history. Tuskegee, Alabama, is the home of Tuskegee University. Two men made this all-black college the pride of African Americans all over the country way back in the late 1800s.

Was Booker T. Washington one of them?

Yes. He was Tuskegee University's first president, and he hired George Washington Carver to come help him. The amazing thing is that both of these famous men were born into slavery and became just about the most important black men of the first half of the twentieth century.

Wow. You know, George Washington Carver—didn't he have something to do with peanuts?

Right again, Maddie! He wanted to help former slaves learn how to be farmers. The soil was very poor from planting cotton year after year, so one of the things he taught them was to plant peanuts. He found more than three hundred ways to use peanuts, in food, medicine, drinks, makeup, you name it!

And I thought they were just for eating!

A. "Hammerin' Hank" Aaron was the first baseball player to get 3,000 career hits and 500 career home runs. He later held the all-time major-league record of 755 home runs for more than thirty years!

Birmingham is the capital here, isn't it? We learned in school that it was built after the Civil War and was the biggest industrial city in the whole South.

Maybe that's why Alabama calls itself "the Heart of Dixie." Dixie is an old-fashioned name for the South.

Am I seeing things? Does that sign say "Space Camp"?

It sure does! It's part of the United States Space and Rocket Center here in Huntsville. You can learn all about space flight: the Saturn V rocket, which helped Apollo put men on the moon, was made right here. There are tons of rocket and missile models to see.

And there's even a ride called Space Shot. This is much better than a camp on an old lake, Josh. Sign me up!

Who is Rosa Parks? Isn't she from Alabama?

Yes, she was a black woman from Montgomery who became famous when she refused to give up her seat on a bus to a white person back in 1955. I guess she's just about the first hero of the civil rights movement. I don't know if I could ever be as brave as she was.

Q. A woman from tiny Monroeville, Alabama, wrote a book that has become one of America's favorites. Who is she and what's the book?

I know it. We can hardly believe now that there was so much racial discrimination back then. Ordinary people like Rosa Parks were what made America change, but it was a long and bitter fight.

I know something fun we can do in this town called Winfield. It's called Mule Day. Come on!

Mule Day? Who cares about a mule?

Well, they do in Alabama. In 1885 Montgomery started a big trolley system for the city and all the cars were drawn by mules. The next year, they electrified it and became the first city in the country with electric streetcars. Now Winfield has a celebration and twenty-five thousand people come every year! There's a mule parade, mule beauty contests, and of course food, dancing, crafts and stuff. I think Alabamans just like to sort of say "thank you" to the hard-working mule!

Hey, do you know what the Iron Bowl is?

It's what they call the annual football game between state archrivals the University of Alabama and Auburn University. Know why it's called the Iron Bowl?

I do. There's lots of iron ore right near Birmingham, which is what's needed to make cast iron and steel. Iron ore is one of Alabama's great natural resources and steel production one of its biggest businesses. As fans say "Go, Crimson Tide!"

A. Harper Lee's 1960 *To Kill a Mockingbird*, about a little girl named Scout's encounter with racial injustice in the 1940s. Harper Lee never wrote another book.

ALASKA

State Capital:	Juneau
Largest City:	Anchorage
Major Industry:	oil (petroleum)
Bordering U.S. States:	none
Bordering Country:	Canada
Bordering Bodies of Water:	Arctic Ocean, Pacific Ocean, Beaufort Sea, Bering Sea, Gulf of Alaska
State Flower:	wild forget-me-not
State Tree:	Sitka spruce
State Sport:	dog mushing
State Nickname:	The Last Frontier
State Motto:	"North to the Future"
State Song:	"Alaska's Flag"

Alaska became the 49th state on January 3, 1959.

North Slope

Mt. McKinley

Iditarod Race

JUNEAU

Inside Passage

Q. Who is Bennie Benson?

You know, Julie, there's a saying, "Everything's bigger in Texas," but the truth is, Alaska takes the cake!

How, Kevin?

Well, it's the biggest of all the fifty states, and it's also home to the highest point in the country—Mount McKinley is 20,320 feet tall! There are also more than 6,600 miles of coastline.

Alaska is so far away from the rest of the states, it's easy to forget how great it is. And remember reading about it in school? When America bought Alaska, everyone called it "Seward's Folly."

Right. William Seward was secretary of state and bought the land for something like two cents an acre. Everyone thought it was crazy.

Well, here's something that *is* kind of crazy.

Juneau is the capital, but you can't drive there.

What th'. . . ?

Yup. You can only get there by airplane or boat. It's on the water, with a gigantic mountain behind. No way anyone could drive to it.

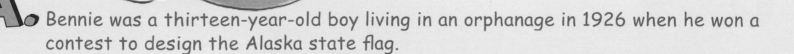

A. Bennie was a thirteen-year-old boy living in an orphanage in 1926 when he won a contest to design the Alaska state flag.

It's no wonder people call Alaska "America's Last Frontier." There's lots of oil here and the Trans-Alaska Pipeline was built in the 1970s to transport it. The pipeline pumps about 400,000 barrels of crude oil a day. The oil and gas industry is really big business in Alaska.

We agree Buster's the best dog ever, right?

Duh! Of course!

Do you think he could win the Iditarod?

Isn't that the big sled dog race? Let's see if we can sign him up! There are sixteen dogs on a team, so he'd have some help. It's really tough: 1,161 miles, all the way from near Anchorage to Nome. It can take two weeks, Kevin!

Mush, Buster! Make us proud!

What do Alaskans do for a living if they don't work in the oil industry?

Well, the fishing industry is huge here. Most of the crab, salmon, herring, and halibut come from these waters.

Parts of Alaska are closer to Russia and Asia than they are to lots of the U.S. states. Many people who are Alaskans are descended from Asian peoples. Inupiat and Yup'ik people are indigenous to Alaska—that means they are native to Alaska. Even today, Alaska Natives and American Indians make up 15 percent of the population. Much of Alaska lies in the Arctic Circle, and although it is extremely cold, global warming seems to be melting some arctic ice.

Who were the explorers who came here? It's pretty remote.

In the 1700s it was the Russians who came first, hunters and fur trappers opening trading posts. But in 1896, the Klondike gold rush began and people from all over the United States came, looking for their fortune.

But who built all these totem poles? I've seen them in old movies.

It's funny: missionaries used to think they honored false gods—but people build totem poles just to tell stories, like weddings, deaths, a family's past, and sometimes to point a finger at a bad neighbor, like a debtor.

In a way, totem poles are like a book!

A. It's the northernmost city in the United States; being in the Arctic Circle, the sun never sets for 82 straight days. It's dark for 51 to 67 days, which is a good time to see the Northern Lights.

ARIZONA

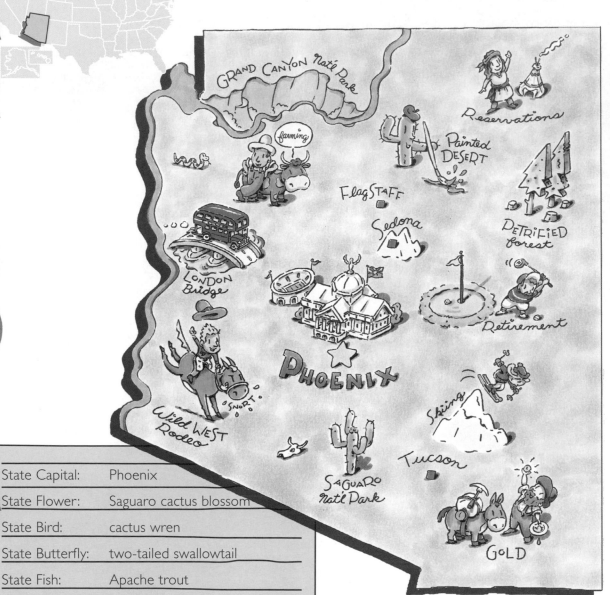

Arizona was the 48th state admitted to the USA on February 14, 1912. The date was also the fiftieth anniversary of Arizona's recognition as a United States territory. Only about 15 percent of Arizona land is privately owned: the rest is Indian reservations, forest and park land, or land held in state trust.

The amount of copper on the roof of the Capitol Building is equivalent to 4,800,000 pennies, which means it is worth $48,000!

State Capital:	Phoenix
State Flower:	Saguaro cactus blossom
State Bird:	cactus wren
State Butterfly:	two-tailed swallowtail
State Fish:	Apache trout
State Mammal:	ringtail
State Reptile:	ridge-nosed rattlesnake
State Gem:	turquoise
State Tree:	palo verde
State Neckwear:	bola tie
State Fossil:	petrified wood
State Nickname:	Grand Canyon State
State Motto:	"Ditat Deus" (God enriches)
State Song:	"Arizona March Song"

Q. Arizona's weather has long prompted people to move here and retire. What business, catering to retirees, started here?

Leo, is this the same Colorado River that's at the top of the Hoover Dam in Nevada? Now it's waaaay down at the bottom of this big canyon?

*G*rand Canyon, you mean, Carri; and yes, it is! Careful! You almost don't see the canyon until you're right on top of it. It's more than a mile deep, and in some places it's more than 18 miles wide. It's one of the Seven Wonders of the Natural World. Over the course of millions of years, the Colorado River, along with ice and wind, has helped carve this out. An explorer named John Wesley Powell was the one who first called it the "Grand Canyon." In 1869, he led nine other people on a trip of 1,000 miles down the Colorado River to the Canyon.

He sounds awfully brave!

You can't even imagine! Major Powell did all this exploration with just one arm; he had lost the other fighting in the Civil War.

What's that gigantic cactus I see, the one with the big arms?

Ao The very first old-age home in America opened for pioneers in Prescott, Arizona, in 1911.

It's called a saguaro, and the tallest one in Arizona is 57 feet 11 inches high, which is taller than most houses! The "arms" don't even begin to grow until the plants are about sixty-five years old, and they can live for one hundred years after that. The saguaro flower blooms at night, only once, and never blooms again. Some birds poke holes in saguaros and make themselves a nesting place.

From this map, it looks like a lot of Arizona is an Indian reservation.

Yep. Almost all of the northeastern part of the state is the Navajo Indian Reservation, or Navajo Nation. It covers 27,000 square miles and goes into parts of Utah and New Mexico. It's the largest area in the country of land set aside for Native Americans. The Apaches are closely related to the Navajos and live there, too, and there's also a smaller Hopi reservation. Many people here make their living doing the same things Native Americans did so long ago: herding sheep and cattle, weaving, and making jewelry.

Q. How is a tepee different from a wigwam?

Hey, I'll bet that's the Painted Desert up ahead.

You can't miss the Painted Desert; it looks like a layer cake in the sunset: the mountains turn red, pink, orange, and purple. Minerals and eons of decaying organic matter are what make them look that way.

Hey, where are those kids going? They just disappeared!

It's called a corn maze, and they're awesome. Do you get the joke? *Maize* was the word Indians used for "corn" back in the Pilgrim days. But this corn maze is something the farmers construct by making paths in the cornfields. You try to see if you can figure out the route and come out the other end.

A. A tepee is a cone-shaped structure of stripped tree saplings covered with cloth. A wigwam is dome-shaped and often covered with natural things such as grass, brush, bark, and reeds.

Is it true that Phoenix, the state capital, is in the desert?

Sure: it's the Sonoran Desert. It covers 120,000 square miles—the entire state of Rhode Island is only 1,545 square miles! It's got lots of exotic plants and animals. There are bobcats, scorpions, black widow spiders, lots of snakes, like the diamondback rattlesnake and the coral snake, and gila monsters, which are really lizards.

Yikes! It sounds scary roaming around so close to so many snakes.

Just watch where you step!

I feel like my watch is wrong. It seems to be getting dark awfully early.

Arizona is the only state in the continental United States that doesn't observe daylight saving time. No one wanted it here! Part of the reason for daylight saving is to give the farmer another hour of light for work. But it's so warm here, people don't want another hour of hot sun!

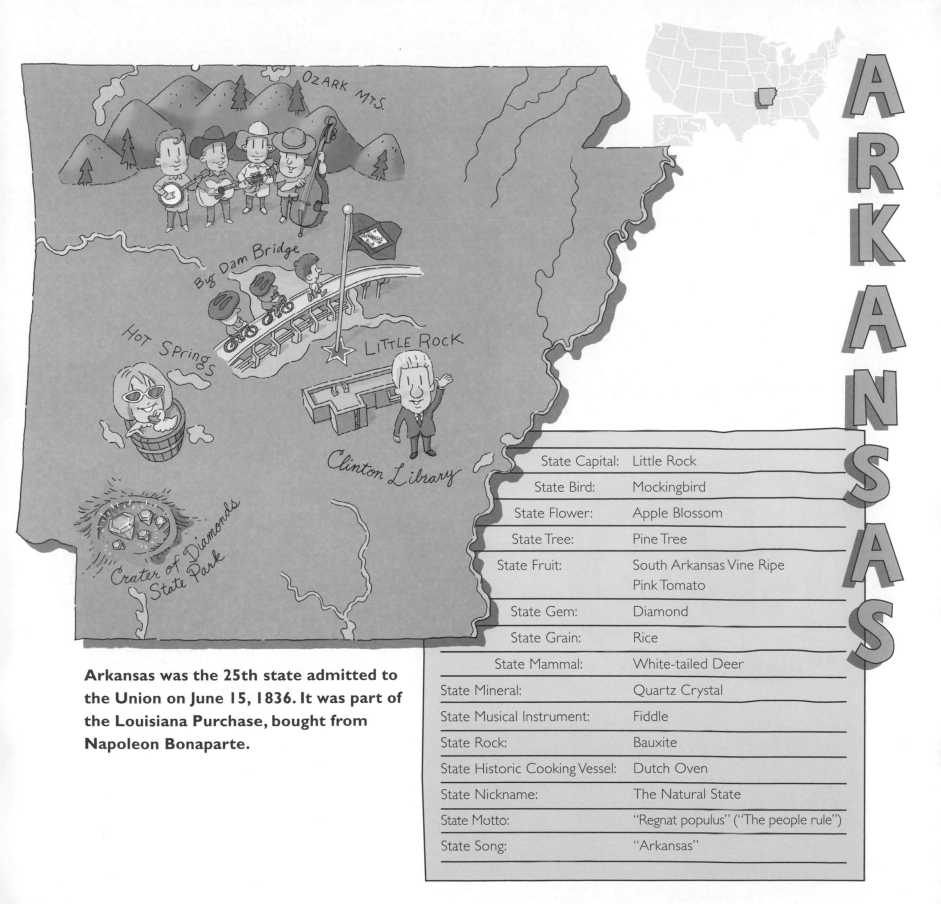

Arkansas was the 25th state admitted to the Union on June 15, 1836. It was part of the Louisiana Purchase, bought from Napoleon Bonaparte.

State Capital:	Little Rock
State Bird:	Mockingbird
State Flower:	Apple Blossom
State Tree:	Pine Tree
State Fruit:	South Arkansas Vine Ripe Pink Tomato
State Gem:	Diamond
State Grain:	Rice
State Mammal:	White-tailed Deer
State Mineral:	Quartz Crystal
State Musical Instrument:	Fiddle
State Rock:	Bauxite
State Historic Cooking Vessel:	Dutch Oven
State Nickname:	The Natural State
State Motto:	"Regnat populus" ("The people rule")
State Song:	"Arkansas"

Here we are in the South, in the state of Arkansas. Believe it or not, settlers came here in the sixteenth century, earlier than the Pilgrims. That isn't as well known because the state wasn't in the thirteen original colonies.

Who explored here, Kevin?

A man from Spain named Hernando de Soto. He was also the first European to discover the Mississippi River. The funny thing is, Julie, he was looking for gold and China.

Wow, was he ever a long way off. But speaking of gold, I've heard that there are diamond mines here in Arkansas.

We should visit a place called Crater of Diamonds State Park. You can keep any jewels you find!

Isn't former president Bill Clinton from Arkansas?

Yup. He was born in a town called Hope, but he grew up in Hot Springs.

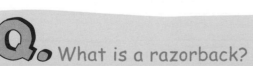

Q. What is a razorback?

Are there hot springs in Hot Springs?

Famous ones. They're waters that come out of the ground, and they're 147 degrees! Folks go to really fancy spas these days, but the springs have been here for ages. Scientists say that the water that comes out today came down as rainfall four thousand years ago! For hundreds of years, Native Americans have come to the springs because they are thought to heal pain and illness. Even famous baseball player Babe Ruth and former president Franklin Delano Roosevelt came here.

It's pretty here. Aren't the Ozark Mountains in Arkansas?

Right, Julie! There's lots of folk art and culture in the Ozarks, too, in towns like Mountain View, which have some awesome festivals. There's even a bean fest and an outhouse race—and of course, lots of local bluegrass music.

I know that Little Rock is Arkansas's capital, and we're just learning in school about desegregation in the 1950s.

You and I can hardly believe it now, but our grandparents can remember when black and white kids weren't allowed to go to the same school together. But the federal government stepped in and escorted nine brave African-American students into the all-white Little Rock High School in 1957. The president sent in the army to protect them.

That was a very important part of the American civil rights movement.

It's a wild boar—sort of like a big, dangerous pig—and also the official name of the University of Arkansas sports team.

While we're in Little Rock, I want to show you something wild. The Big Dam Bridge is almost a mile long, but it's only 14 feet wide.

Wow! I guess it's only for people walking or riding bikes.

It connects more than 14 miles of biking and hiking trails all over Little Rock.

Let's get our bikes!

Here's a small town that produced one of the biggest businessmen America has ever known: Bentonville, the home of Sam Walton and Wal-Mart. He started with a tiny discount store. It just shows even the littlest guy can succeed big.

There sure is lots of farmland. What's growing in Arkansas?

Well, you could almost say . . . dinner! It's number one in production of chicken and rice. But also cotton, soybeans, and grapes are all grown here.

And I see signs everywhere about parks.

Because there are six National Park sites, thirteen major lakes, two mountain ranges for hiking, and more than 9,000 miles of streams and rivers to fish and canoe in. That's why we call it "the Natural State." First one to grab a paddle, wins!

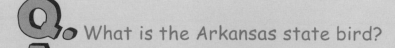

Q. What is the Arkansas state bird?

A. The mockingbird, which is able to mimic other birds, animals, and even things like car alarms! They often do this to protect their territory.

California was the 31st state admitted to the USA on September 9, 1850. It is so physically long that the economy and political issues of the northern part of the state often seem very different from those in the southern portion.

A politician named Joseph Spinney was so corrupt that he only lasted as mayor of Fresno for ten minutes!

State Capital:	Sacramento
State Bird:	California Valley quail
State Animal:	California grizzly bear
State Flower:	golden poppy
State Tree:	California redwood
State Fish:	California golden trout
State Marine Fish:	garibaldi
State Marine Mammal:	California gray whale
State Prehistoric Artifact:	chipped stone bear
State Reptile:	desert tortoise
State Gold Rush Ghost Town:	Bodie
State Silver Rush Ghost Town:	Calico
State Tall Ship:	*Californian*
State Nickname:	Golden State
State Motto:	"Eureka—I have found it"
State Song:	"I Love You, California"

GIANT REDWOODS

THE GOLD RUSH of 1849!

SIERRA NEVADA

LAKE TAHOE

SACRAMENTO

NAPA VALLEY

San Joaquin Valley

MTS.

San Francisco

Oakland

San Jose

YOSEMITE PARK

SILICON VALLEY

DEATH VALLEY

HOLLYWOOD

MOJAVE DESERT

Los Angeles

San Diego

Palm Springs

CALIFORNIA

Wow, I wish my mom could see me now—I'm in Hollywood!

Easy, Rick. You don't even have an agent yet!

But I love it already. How did the movie business wind up here, Carla?

Well, the first Hollywood movie studios came to California in the early 1900s. The sunshine provided good lighting and great weather for filming. Pretty soon it was the most important place in the world for making movies.

And Hollywood is part of Los Angeles, right?

Exactly. Los Angeles, L.A., La-La Land—it's really a collection of smaller cities, including Beverly Hills, Pasadena, Long Beach, and Santa Monica. There are 14 million people all together, with 3.5 million in the city itself. If Los Angeles were a country, its economy would be larger than Switzerland's! And more immigrants come here than to any other city in the United States. In the olden days, coming from the east over the

Q. What's the official state dance of California?

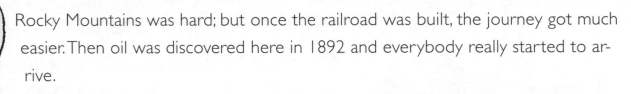

Rocky Mountains was hard; but once the railroad was built, the journey got much easier. Then oil was discovered here in 1892 and everybody really started to arrive.

I bet you'll tell me the next big industry was computers.

You got it! Welcome to Silicon Valley, which technology has made it one of the wealthiest areas in the world.

What's silicon, anyway?

It's a basic element used in silicon chips, which is an important part of computers. Stretching from San Jose to Palo Alto, Silicon Valley got its start as a technological mecca in 1938 when two Stanford University graduates, William Hewlitt and David Packard, began an electronics workshop in a garage. Hewlitt-Packard became one of the largest electronics manufacturers in the world. In the 1970s, Steve Jobs invented the modern computer and started Apple—and you know the rest!

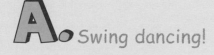

A. Swing dancing!

Man, San Francisco sure is beautiful.

The steep hills, handsome buildings, morning fog, ocean air, and picturesque San Francisco Bay—complete with the Golden Gate Bridge—make it "Everyone's Favorite City." But it wasn't always that way.

In the late 1700s, San Francisco was little more than a small religious community. Then in 1848, boom! Gold was discovered in the mountains nearby and everything changed. Most people didn't find gold, though, and by the mid-twentieth century, it became a center for people with new political ideas and others who were seeking alternative lifestyles.

Back up, Carla. Wasn't there a famous earthquake in San Francisco a long time ago?

To tell you the truth, Rick, there have been a few. The San Andreas Fault that runs north to south through California caused the 1906 San Francisco Earthquake and several others since then, both here and in Los Angeles. Some people won't live in California because of the chance of earthquakes.

But it's so pretty here! How could they resist?

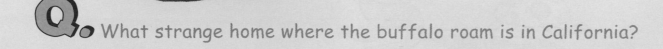

Q. What strange home where the buffalo roam is in California?

As you can imagine, since California is so big, it has some pretty strange geography.

Like what?

Well, it goes from Mount Whitney, the highest mountain peak in the continental United States at 14,494 feet, to the infamous Death Valley.

Eek! Sounds scary.

It can be. Badwater, at the bottom of Death Valley, is 282 feet below sea level. It's so hot you could fry an egg on the hood of your car. But we could drive back into the mountains and quick-freeze it in a snowbank! It's gotten as high as 134°F in Death Valley.

I guess I know where the valley got its name! But isn't California known more for its trees?

Yes, it is best know for the Sequoia sempervirens or California redwood. There are whole forests of these trees in our state. Some are 2,200 years old and almost 400 feet high!

Wow, California is a wild place, Carla. You're right—it's got it all!

A. Catalina Island! Several were brought there in 1924 during the filming of a movie, and were left to live off the land. Today there are more than 150 still on the island.

COLORADO

Colorado is called "the Centennial State" because it became our 38th state just a few weeks after America's hundredth birthday, on August 1, 1876. Colorado's southwest corner is part of the "Four Corners" along with New Mexico, Arizona, and Utah; it is the only place in the United States where four states meet at one place.

In 1945, a Fruita, Colorado, farmer cut the head off a young rooster, planning on a delicious dinner. But "Mike the Headless Wonder Chicken" lived . . . for eighteen months! Every year the town has an entire Mike Festival!

State Capital:	Denver
Area:	At 104,100 square miles, Colorado is our eighth largest state.
Highest Point:	Mount Elbert is the highest peak in the Rocky Mountains, at 14,433 feet.
State Animal:	Rocky Mountain bighorn sheep
State Bird:	lark bunting
State Fish:	greenback cutthroat trout
State Flower:	white and lavender columbine
State Insect:	Colorado hairstreak butterfly
State Reptile:	western painted turtle
State Tree:	Colorado blue spruce

Q. Who was Katherine Lee Bates?

C'mon, there's gold in them thar hills!

Beau, you've been watching too much TV!

Well, there was gold, Penny, and lots of it. Didn't you ever hear of the Pikes Peak gold rush? Over 100,000 people came here in covered wagons starting in 1859, trying to find their fortune.

Did some people get rich?

Sure, lots of them. Not only that, but many of the people who came to find gold settled here in what became Colorado. Boulder and even Denver, Colorado's biggest city and capital, started as mining camps during the rush.

Are there any gold mines today?

Yes, but they find the gold now with huge machinery, of course. Silver mining is very big here, too. There are even places you can go panning for gold.

Well, what's the holdup? You get some mules, I'll get the pans and pickaxes! We're going to be rich!

Oh, brother. It's pretty interesting, though, to think that's how so many people ended up coming out here.

That's true, but I'll bet those old prospectors and other frontiersmen could never have guessed what brings people here now: skiing!

 She was a songwriter who, when she took a sightseeing trip on a mule up to Pikes Peak, found it so breathtaking that she sat right down and wrote the words to "America the Beautiful."

This is maybe the best state for skiing in the entire country, with Vail, Aspen, and Breckenridge, just to name a few

Makes me want to sing, "Rocky Mountain Hiiiiigh, Colorado!"

Ouch! That's the state song—I'm sure no one ever wanted to hear John Denver's song sound that way. Skipper's howling!

Where did the word "Colorado" even come from?

It means "colored red" in Spanish. Think about our trip to Pikes Peak—remember how the soil is so reddish up there? Colorado is the highest state in the country. They call Denver "the Mile-High City" because it's a whole mile above sea level. The air up here can even make you dizzy, because it has less oxygen.

There are plenty of fun things to do here. Of course there's skiing, and snowboarding, and wicked good trout fishing, but my dad's been whitewater rafting, too, down the Colorado River—it goes all the way through the Grand Canyon in Arizona.

Q. What is "Beulah red" marble?

I want to show you something you won't believe, at a National Park called Mesa Verde. It's someplace people used to live, around eight hundred years ago.

So I guess it's not a fancy ski chalet?

No, it sure isn't. They're called cliff dwellings and Native Americans called the Anasazi lived here. Mesa Verde wasn't even discovered until a little more than a hundred years ago; they had been empty all that time. There are more than six hundred pueblos, made with stone, poles, and adobe, or clay.

They are the awesomest thing I've ever seen. I like to picture what it was like when it was a village, with people everywhere.

I'm guessing you haven't seen Balanced Rock, either.

Whoa! That thing is definitely going to fall over!

Ha! Maybe one day, but not while we're alive. It also depends on which angle you look at it from— it's sort of an optical illusion. Over the centuries, weaker layers of rock have eroded at the bottom, but I promise you, it's very strong!

A. It's a local stone whose real name is Colorado rose onyx. It is so beautiful and rare that all known quantities were used in building the Colorado State Capitol.

CONNECTICUT

The Hartford Courant is the oldest U.S. newspaper that is still being published today. The printing presses started rolling in 1764.

HARTFORD

Mark Twain HOUSE

MYSTIC Seaport

BEARDSLEY ZOO

P.T. Barnum MUSEUM

ESSEX Railroad MUSEUM

Dutch traders sailed up the Connecticut River in 1614, landing near what is now Hartford. A few small groups made their homes nearby, but the city of Hartford wasn't founded until 1636. The name "Connecticut" originates from the Mohegan Indian word *quinnitukqut,* which means "beside the long tidal river."

State Capital:	Hartford
Date Entered the Union:	Jan. 9, 1788
State Bird:	American robin
State Flower:	mountain laurel
State Mammal:	sperm whale
State Tree:	charter white oak
State Dance:	square dance
State Fossil:	dinosaur tracks
State Mineral:	garnet
State Shell:	Eastern oyster
State Slogan:	"Full of surprises"
State Song:	"Yankee Doodle"

Q. What book was published in New Haven in 1878?

Where are we, Scott? I feel like someone has put me in a time machine.

Ha! I guess *I* sort of did. This is Mystic Seaport, Connecticut, and the folks here call it a maritime museum. It's a reproduction of a seafaring village in the 1800s. Isn't it awesome?

Totally. What's that huge boat?

Something *that* big is called a ship, Elsa. It's the *Charles W. Morgan*, and it's an actual whaling ship—in fact, the only one left in America. We can even climb onboard.

I'M HISTORIC!

SO AM I!

The other ship there is a recreation of the *Amistad*, a schooner that was filled with African slaves bought by a rich man in Cuba. The slaves rose up and took over the ship. An important legal case set them all free; this was almost twenty-five years before slavery was abolished by Abraham Lincoln.

Scott, why do the people here act so differently?

Mystic is what's called a living history museum, meaning everyone acts as if they are actually people living in this village back in the old days. It makes it feel real.

A. The very first telephone book was put out by the New Haven District Telephone Company. It only listed fifty names!

Being in New England, Connecticut must have been one of our first states.

Yup, the fifth, to be exact—it's called "the Constitution State." Many historians believe Connecticut's Fundamental Orders of 1638 were the basis for the U.S. Constitution, even though that was written almost 150 years later.

IT FLYS!

Hmmm. Well, it's better than their other state nickname, "the Land of Steady Habits." That's pretty boring!

You're right. But it's not boring here at all. People here do all kinds of interesting things, like building nuclear submarines. Igor Sikorsky built the first mass-produced helicopter here, too, in 1942. There are even museums for both of them here.

Hey, that *is* cool.

Naturally, the people in Connecticut do other things to make a living, too—not everybody builds helicopters! The insurance industry began here, mostly around Hartford, the capital. And there are flower nurseries, poultry and dairy products, and cattle, which make Connecticut and its citizens very successful.

What's that sign that says P. T. Barnum? Does he have anything to do with the circus?

Yes, it's the Barnum Museum. He started out as a politician and businessman. He didn't even start his

Q. What's odd about the New London Ledge Lighthouse?

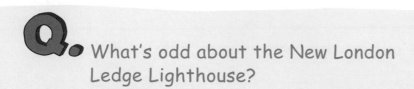

circus, which he called "the Greatest Show on Earth," until he was sixty-one!
He even bought his own train, so he could take it all over the country.
He is just one of Connecticut's famous folks.

Really? Like who else?

Well, Nathan Hale, for one: he's the State
Hero. He fought in the Revolutionary War,
remember?

Sure. Isn't he the one that said, "I only
regret that I have but one life to give to
my country?"

That's him. There's someone else who even now helps us every day,
named Noah Webster. Know why?

He wrote *Webster's Dictionary*!
I have my own.

It took him twenty-seven
years to write it and he
had to learn more than
two dozen languag-
es to do it.

I'll bet he also
knew Connecti-
cut's state motto—"full
of surprises"—just like the state!

A. Aside from the fact that it's allegedly haunted by Ernie, one of its former keep-
ers, it looks nothing like a regular lighthouse, but a fancy home one might have
found onshore around 1909, when it was built.

DELAWARE

State Capital:	Dover
State Bird:	Blue Hen Chicken
State Flower:	Peach Blossom
State Tree:	American Holly
State Fish:	Weakfish
State Fossil:	Belemnite
State Herb:	Sweet Goldenrod
State Dessert:	Peach Pie
State Macroinvertebrate:	Stonefly
State Marine Animal:	Horseshoe Crab
State Song:	"Our Delaware,"
State Star:	Delaware Diamond, located in the constellation of Ursa Major
State Nickname:	First State, Diamond State, Blue Hen State, Small Wonder
State Motto:	"Liberty and Independence"
State Song:	"Our Delaware"

Delaware became the 1st state on December 7, 1787. It is the second smallest state, and has only three counties!

WINTERHUR

GREENVILLE

BATTLE of COOCH'S BRIDGE

DOVER

Rehoboth Beach

Fenwick Island

Q. What's on the Delaware state seal?

40

ell, George, I guess it wouldn't be hard to guess why Delaware is called "the First State."

Not really, Mimi. Was Delaware the first state to sign the Constitution?

You got it: on December 7, 1787. It seems the people of Delaware have always worked hard to make sure America even *happened.* Take a look at the back of this Delaware state quarter: that's Caesar Rodney.

Who's he?

A politician who was president of Delaware when it was still a colony. He was so committed to our independence as a nation that he rode 80 miles on horseback during a terrible thunderstorm to break a tied vote and sign the Declaration of Independence.

Yikes! He *was* dedicated. Where did Delaware get its name, though?

It's complicated. Virginia's first colonial governor was named Thomas West, third Baron De La Warr. Actually, the Delaware River was named after him first, and then the state, which is sort of crazy since he lived in Virginia.

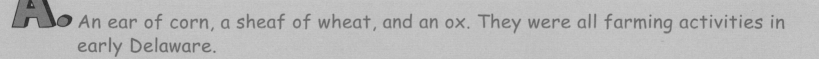

A. An ear of corn, a sheaf of wheat, and an ox. They were all farming activities in early Delaware.

What are these signs that say "Dalmarva"? That's not a word.

It's the way to the beach! The Delmarva Peninsula is made up of three states.

Let me guess: Delaware, Maryland, and Virginia!

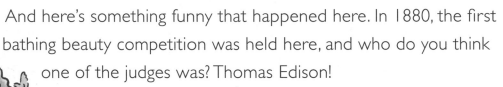

And here's Rehoboth Beach, Delaware—my favorite. It's a tiny town; but in the summer, tons of people come, including some from Washington DC, where there's no beach at all.

Wow! Check out this boardwalk—games, hotels, souvenirs, food—it's got it all!

And here's something funny that happened here. In 1880, the first bathing beauty competition was held here, and who do you think one of the judges was? Thomas Edison!

The great inventor? No way!

I keep seeing signs everywhere that say Du Pont. What's that?

It started as a little gunpowder mill in 1802, near Wilmington. The Du Pont family had come here to escape the French Revolution. Today it's the second largest chemical company in the world. They make things like nylon, Teflon, Lycra—even Kevlar, the material for bulletproof vests.

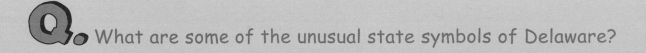

Q. What are some of the unusual state symbols of Delaware?

And that big mansion, Winterthur?

That was a Du Pont home. It has some of the most beautiful gardens in the country.

Look at what else they have: it's called Americana, a collection of all sorts of things like tools, postcards, toys, flags, everything! My mother calls my things junk, but here at Winterthur, they say it's very valuable!

And a skylight would be nice, too!

Speaking of houses, did you know the first log cabins in America were built here? I always think of Abe Lincoln, but when settlers from Finland and Sweden arrived in the 1600s, they built log cabins. It took very few tools to make them, there was plenty of wood around, and they could build them in about two days.

There's so much history here—I love that. Was much of the American Revolution fought here? It was after all, "the First State."

That's the funny thing. There was only one battle in that war ever fought in Delaware: the Battle of Cooch's Bridge, near Newark. But something really special happened there, even though it was barely more than a skirmish: it was the first time America's Stars and Stripes were flown in a battle!

 The American holly is the State Tree, the ladybug the State Bug, and the blue hen chicken the State Bird!

FLORIDA

Florida was the 27th state admitted to the Union on March 3, 1845. Explorer Ponce de Leon claimed the territory in the late 1400s, in his search for the Fountain of Youth. It has a hot, often muggy, climate, but when air-conditioning became readily available in the mid-twentieth century, its population soared. Land was cheap and sun was plentiful!

Gatorade was named for the University of Florida Gators, where the drink was first developed.

PLANTATIONS
JACKSONVILLE
TALLAHASSEE
ORANGE GROVES
DAYTONA
Kennedy Space Center
Tampa
ORLANDO
BEACHES
GATORS
Lake Okeechobee
FT. LAUDERDALE
MIAMI
The Keys

State Capital:	Tallahassee
State Bird:	mockingbird
State Flower:	orange blossom
State Wildflower:	coreopsis
State Animal:	Florida panther
State Beverage:	orange juice
State Freshwater Fish:	largemouth bass
State Fruit:	orange
State Tree:	sabal palmetto palm
State Marine Mammal:	manatee
State Pie:	Key lime pie
State Reptile:	American alligator
State Rodeo:	Silver Spurs Rodeo
State Saltwater Fish:	Atlantic sailfish
State Saltwater Mammal:	porpoise
State Shell:	horse conch
State Stone:	agatized coral
State Nickname:	Sunshine State
State Motto:	"In God we trust"
State Song:	"The Swanee River" ("Old Folks at Home")
State Anthem:	"Florida, Where the Sawgrass Meets the Road"

Q. Where is the shark tooth capital of the world?

This'll shock you, Chris—I'm about to show you the oldest permanent settlement in the USA.

In Florida, Anita? What about Plymouth?

Nope. There were Native Americans here about ten thousand years ago. By the time Spaniard Juan Ponce de Leon, the first European to land here, arrived, there were already 100,000 Native Americans in Florida. It was Ponce de Leon who named the area "Florida," which means "land of flowers" in Spanish. And millions of years ago, gigantic glaciers covered most of the continent—except Florida. Many animals fled and found themselves here: giant, hairy mastodons and ferocious saber-toothed tigers. Even camels, wolves, and of course, alligators, found their way to Florida.

I guess alligators and Florida sort of go hand in hand!

True! Saint Augustine is home to the "World's Original Alligator Farm." Founded in 1893, it's the only place you can see all twenty-three species of crocodilians in one place.

That's a lot of choppers!

A. Venice, Florida, where on the beach you can find shark teeth as long as 3 inches.

I have to ask: when can we go to Disney World?

How about right now? Walt Disney bought thousands of acres south of Orlando in the 1960s to build his dream amusement park. Ten million people came in the first year, 1971, and now it's the number one tourist destination on earth! The monorails people use to get around the park have traveled enough to go to the moon and back twenty-five times! We don't have time for everything, so we've got to choose which Disney theme park to go to: Animal Kingdom, Disney-MGM Studios, Epcot Center, or the Magic Kingdom.

Magic Kingdom—I want to meet Mickey Mouse. Then Epcot, because it's so high-tech.

Now, how about a day at the beach?

Awesome!

With 1,300 miles of shoreline, Florida has some of the best beaches in the world. And the sand is perfect for sand castles. People have built them as tall as a five-story building. Probably the most famous beach is Daytona Beach. It's 23 miles long, 500

Q. What three towns in Florida are named after planets?

feet wide, and lures more than 8 million visitors a year. They even used to have car races on the flat beach.

But now the Daytona 500 is at the Daytona International Speedway, right?

You got it. How about a stop in my hometown, Miami? More than half the people here were born in a foreign country! My parents came from Cuba, an island only 90 miles from Key West, but I was born here.

The home of the famous South Beach!

Right! It's only twenty-three blocks long, but it's hopping 24/7. The buildings are painted in lollipop colors, with interesting architecture and bright neon signs. You'll see models, muscle-bound Rollerbladers, movie stars, and photo shoots. They call it "the American Riviera," because it's such a fashionable resort area.

A. Jupiter, Venus, and Neptune Beach.

I've seen the Everglades in movies and TV shows. Can we see them?

Oh, you'll love this. There's a 99-mile boating trail from Flamingo to Everglades City that's a real adventure. The Everglades is a very tough place for humans to survive. Many Seminole Indians once lived here, in houses built on stilts called *chickees*.

Why are all these islands called the Florida Keys?

"Key" comes from the Spanish word *cayo*, which means "small island." Key West, my favorite, is at the end of Route 1 and is the southernmost point in the United States.

Look! These signs say MILE 0!

In the 1800s, Key West was the wealthiest community in Florida—most of the money came from salvaged treasure ships!

It's a ton of fun here: fishing, boating, swimming—and we can see the former house of Key West's most famous resident, novelist Ernest Hemingway. The descendants of his famous six-toed cats still roam around—there are over sixty of them!

Like they say here, "It's just another day in paradise!"

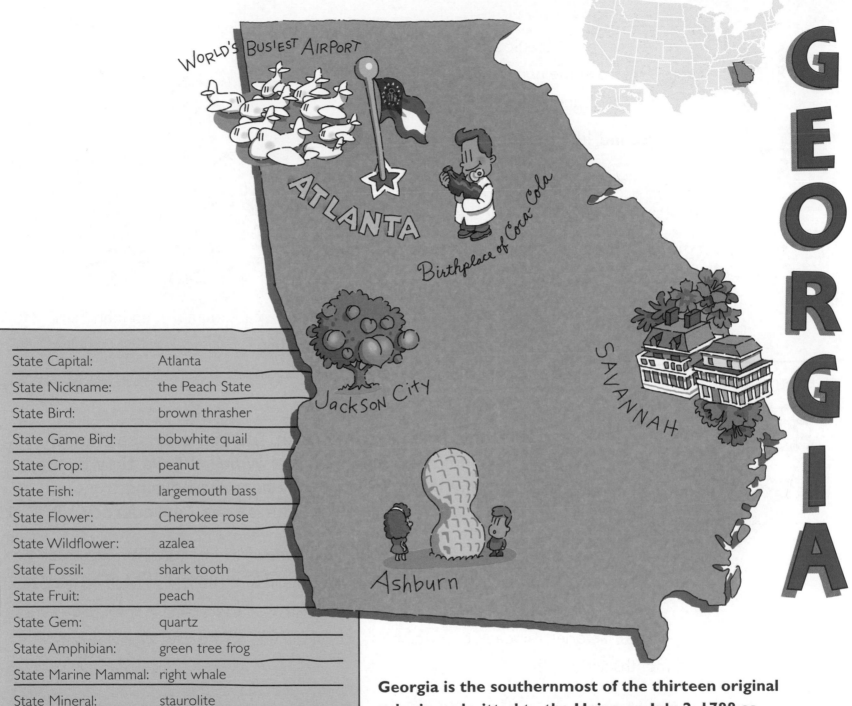

GEORGIA

State Capital:	Atlanta
State Nickname:	the Peach State
State Bird:	brown thrasher
State Game Bird:	bobwhite quail
State Crop:	peanut
State Fish:	largemouth bass
State Flower:	Cherokee rose
State Wildflower:	azalea
State Fossil:	shark tooth
State Fruit:	peach
State Gem:	quartz
State Amphibian:	green tree frog
State Marine Mammal:	right whale
State Mineral:	staurolite
State Motto:	"Wisdom, Justice, Moderation"
State Seashell:	knobbed whelk
State Song:	"Georgia on My Mind"
State Tree:	live oak
State Vegetable:	Vidalia sweet onion

WORLD'S BUSIEST AIRPORT

ATLANTA

Birthplace of Coca-Cola

Jackson City

SAVANNAH

Ashburn

Georgia is the southernmost of the thirteen original colonies, admitted to the Union on July 2, 1788 as the fourth state to ratify the Constitution. It seceded during the Civil War, and was the last state to be restored to the Union, on July 15, 1870.

Hey, y'all, welcome to the South and the great state of Georgia. We're in the home of the three *P*s— peanuts, pecans, and peaches.

Really? Sound like a delicious state to me!

No kidding, Julie! Georgia grows more of all three than anywhere else in the country.

Wow, Georgia is full of culinary surprises. You know that Coca-Cola was invented here, right?

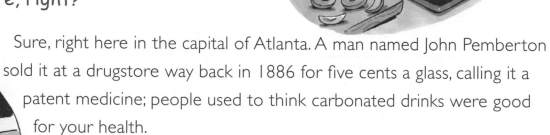

Sure, right here in the capital of Atlanta. A man named John Pemberton sold it at a drugstore way back in 1886 for five cents a glass, calling it a patent medicine; people used to think carbonated drinks were good for your health.

That's pretty funny, Kevin. Did you ever see that old movie called *Gone with the Wind*? Where they burned down Atlanta? That really happened during the Civil War, when Georgia was part of the Confederacy.

In real life, it was just like the movie: General William Tecumseh Sherman marched his troops into Atlanta in 1864. His March to the Sea went all the way to Savannah, and his troops destroyed everything in their path— homes, factories, railroads, everything. After that, the end to the Civil War was only months away.

Qo What is grits?

Oh, Kevin, there's this place I want to go to in Atlanta. It's called Stone Mountain Park, and they have this awesome thing you can do called Sky Hike. You're way up in the treetops, climbing suspended wooden bridges, balancing on one little rope, climbing net bridges—can you imagine?

It sounds scary!

Don't worry—you'll have on safety straps. It'll be exciting! There's a gondola ride we can take while we're there. It gets right up close to the famous Confederate Memorial Carving.

Wow, it's got Jefferson Davis, the president of the Confederacy, General Robert E. Lee, and Stonewall Jackson.

A. Grits is a food made by Native Americans hundred of years ago. It is ground corn and is often served hot with butter at breakfast. In 2002, Georgia made it their Official Prepared Food!

I say we go treasure hunting.

What? Where?

Blackbeard Island, of course! Blackbeard the pirate, whose real name was Edward Teach, lived on this island more than two hundred years ago. The navy owned it, and then for a long time, yellow fever patients were quarantined here. Now it's a nature preserve. For centuries, everyone said there's buried treasure here, and I think we should try to find it!

You're crazy. But let's go!

It's near Savannah, one of the prettiest cities you could ever see. You would never know there had been a war here.

Lots of great people came from Savannah, too. Johnny Mercer was one of the greatest songwriters of all time.

And Flannery O'Connor, one of the greatest Southern writers ever. C'mon, let's take a horse and carriage tour—maybe he can drop us off at Paula Deen's restaurant. All this sightseeing is making me hungry!

Q. What is the Masters Tournament?

You know, there's one U.S. president from Georgia: Jimmy Carter. And he was a peanut farmer from a town named Plains!

People made jokes about that then, but President Carter has become famous for his work with Habitat for Humanity. He even won the Nobel Peace Prize for his work helping to keep peace in the Middle East.

OK, one more stop, but I'm not sure you're going to like it. It's the Whigam's Rattlesnake Roundup.

OK. No way.

It's great. Everyone goes through the nearby woods and spends all day catching snakes. Then there's fried rattlesnake to eat later, and lots of awesome souvenirs, even fangs for sale.

You go right ahead, Julie. I'm going back to Paula Deen's for dessert!

 It is one of the most prestigious golf tournaments of the world, played each year at the Augusta National Gold Club. The winner always gets to sport the famous green blazer when he wins.

HAWAII

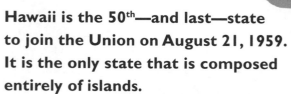

Hawaii is the 50th—and last—state to join the Union on August 21, 1959. It is the only state that is composed entirely of islands.

State Capital:	Honolulu
State Bird:	Nene, also known as the Hawaiian Goose
State Flower:	Pua Aloalo, or Ma`o-hau-hele (Hibiscus brackenridgei)
State Tree:	Kukui Tree
State Dance:	Hula
State Fish:	Humuhumunukunukuapua`a, also known as the rectangular trigger fish
State Gem:	Black Coral
State Individual Sport:	Surfing
State Team Sport:	Outrigger Canoe Paddling
State Mammal:	Hawaiian monk seal
State Marine Mammal:	Humpback Whale
State Nickname:	The Aloha State
State Song:	"Hawai`i Pono`I"

Q. What's different about the Hawaiian island of Nihau?

You know what's funny, Elsa? In so many states you travel to, especially the thirteen original colonies, everything is history, history, history.

I'll bet I know what you're going to say: everything in Hawaii is geography, geography, geography. I feel like just about everything I want to see is outdoors.

Me, too! Hey, I'll bet you didn't know this: Alaska and Hawaii became our newest states so close together that there was just one year when there was a forty-nine-star flag!

My grandma has one in her collection. Hawaii is the last, though, becoming a state on August 21, 1959.

Cowabunga!

NUMBER 50!

What's that mean, Scott? Bart Simpson says it all the time. Snoopy does, too.

It's surfer talk! When the weather's great and you're totally stoked and the waves are huge . . . "cowabunga!"

Wait, that guy who made surfing so popular was Hawaiian, right?

Yup! Duke Kahanamoku. He was an Olympic swimmer back in 1912. Duke grew up near Waikiki Beach where he learned to both swim and surf. He was in the movies, too, and was even the long-time sheriff of Honolulu. He pretty much invented the sport of modern surfing.

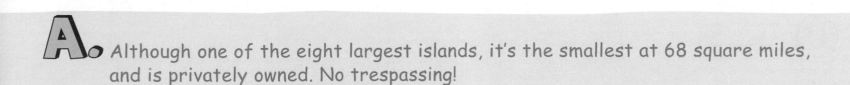

A. Although one of the eight largest islands, it's the smallest at 68 square miles, and is privately owned. No trespassing!

I get confused about all the islands in Hawaii, which were formed by volcanoes. I think I read that Hawaii is an archipelago, which is an island group. How many islands are there?

Good question—and more geography! There are hundreds of little islands that make up the state, but the biggest are the ones we usually talk about: The Big Island, which is also called Hawaii, Maui, Lanai, Molokai, Oahu, and Kauai.

Yipes. I can hardly say them, never mind remember them.

Well, let's visit a couple—that should help!

I do know this: Hawaii is the most isolated place in the world that is so populated. It's almost 2,500 miles from California, the closest other state, and almost 4,000 miles from Japan and 5,000 from China.

It's no wonder, then, that Hawaiians have their own language. Even though most kids today speak English, lots of them know how to speak Hawaiian, too. There are only twelve letters in the Hawaiian alphabet!

Wow! Let's get back to the different islands. Honolulu is the capital and that's on Oahu, right?

Q. Hawaii has produced only one United States president—who is he?

Right. "The Big Island" is called Hawaii, too. It's known for its active volcanoes and is the largest island in the United States. Maui is the second largest; a lot of the pineapple, macadamia nuts, and coffee Hawaii's known for come from here. Loads of tourists like to come and drive along the Hana Highway. You can go to the famous Haleakal National Park and see the cool volcano, the Haleakaia Crater—don't worry, it's not active! People come from all over the world to see the sunrises here.

What about Molokai? Isn't that where Father Damien was?

Yes. He was a priest who went to the island, part of which was a leper colony. After many years of great work, he contracted the disease himself and died.

We'll never have time to go to all the islands, Scott. What's a great thing we could see that's *not* outdoors?

The royal palace!

What? The United States has a president, not a king.

That's true now, but until 1893, Hawaii had kings and queens who lived right here in Iolani Palace in Honolulu. It's a museum now, but I sure wouldn't mind living here!

A. Barack Obama (1961–), also America's first African-American president, grew up in Honolulu.

IDAHO

State Capital:	Boise
State Bird:	mountain bluebird
State Flower:	syringa
State Fossil:	Hagerman horse fossil
State Fruit:	huckleberry
State Horse:	Appaloosa
State Insect:	monarch butterfly
State Raptor:	peregrine falcon
State Nickname:	the Gem State
State Motto:	"Esto Perpetua" ("Let it be forever")
State Song:	"Here We Have Idaho"
State Tree:	white pine
State Vegetable:	potato

Idaho became the 43rd state on July 3, 1890. It is located in the Pacific Northwest.

LEWIS & CLARK

SODA SPRINGS GEYSER

BOISE

Trout Fishing Capitol of the World

Buhl

SHOSHONE FALLS

Blackfoot Potato Museum

Q. What famous author lived, wrote and fished in Ketchum, the town where Sun Valley resort is located?

Υou can't think about Idaho without thinking about potatoes.

I think about french fries especially. I happen to know that one-third of all the potatoes Americans eat are from Idaho.

> I can be mashed, hashed, chipped, baked and fried!

True—but there's so much more to know! How about this: we can go mine for the state gem, the star garnet. Idaho is named "the Gem State" because almost every gem has been found here, but the star garnet is only found here and in India. Sometimes they're as big as a golf ball.

Wow! Let's go mining—I want to find one for my mom.

After that, let's go skiing at Sun Valley. It was the first major ski resort in the United States, opening way back in 1936. W. Averell Harriman, who owned the Union Pacific Railroad, figured he'd get more people to ride the train if he built a winter paradise here. He was one of the first to popularize skiing in America. The rail company even invented the chair lift. Before that, people just used rope tows. Harriman and his crew got the idea from equipment used to load bananas onto fruit ships!

A. Ernest Hemingway wrote such famous books as *A Farewell to Arms*, *For Whom the Bell Tolls*, and *The Sun Also Rises*. He won the Nobel Prize for Literature for his work.

I know someone who lived in Idaho who changed everyone's life forever: Philo T. Farnsworth.

Never heard of him. What does he have to do with me?

How about this, Josh? He invented the television.

THERE'S NOTHING TO WATCH!

Oh. Well, maybe you're right. Tell me more.

He was born in a log cabin in 1906, and then his family moved to Rigby, Idaho, to farm. He couldn't believe it when he found the farm had electricity to run its machinery. Even as a kid he was a genius with electronics, fixing things around the house. He was only twenty-one when he invented an image dissector, which transmitted a picture electronically.

I know they grow a lot of wheat in Idaho, and that lumber and food processing are big industries, but I think Philo would be proud: today what Idaho is most successful at is science and technology, lots of it centered around Boise, the capital.

Q. What is an Appaloosa?

Sports like skiing and fly-fishing draw lots of tourists. And, of course, the biggest sand dune in the country is in Idaho.

That's crazy.

I'm not kidding! Bruneau Dunes has a dune that's 470 feet high! Scientists think they formed after a flood about fifteen thousand years ago. You're even allowed to sled and ride horses on them!

OK, if you're so smart, what are those jaggedy mountains over there?

The Sawtooth Mountains! They have just about every outdoor sport: rock climbing, hiking, camping, kayaking, mountain biking, you name it!

Don't get me wrong, I love TV, but I believe Philo T. Farnsworth would agree: Idaho is the most fun outside!

A. It's a beautiful horse that's spotted like a leopard, and is the State Horse of Idaho. Native Americans called the Nez Percé are responsible for the American breed. Patterned horses like the Appaloosa were even coach horses for Louis XIV of France!

ILLINOIS

Illinois was the 21st state in the USA; it became a state on December 3, 1818.

Abraham Lincoln, Ulysses S. Grant, and Barack Obama are all presidents who were elected while living in Illinois. Aside from these famous men, we have John Deere to thank for inventing the steel plow that made Illinois's prairie one of the most fertile planting grounds in the country.

The vehicles of Illinois residents sport the highest number of personalized license plates in the USA.

State Capital:	Springfield
State Flower:	native violet
State Bird:	cardinal
State Tree:	white oak
State Animal:	white-tailed deer
State Fruit:	GoldRush apple
State Reptile:	painted turtle
State Amphibian:	eastern tiger salamander
State Fish:	bluegill
State Prairie Grass:	big bluestem
State Snack:	popcorn
State Slogan:	"Land of Lincoln"
State Nickname:	Prairie State
State Motto:	"State Sovereignty, National Union"
State Song:	"Illinois"

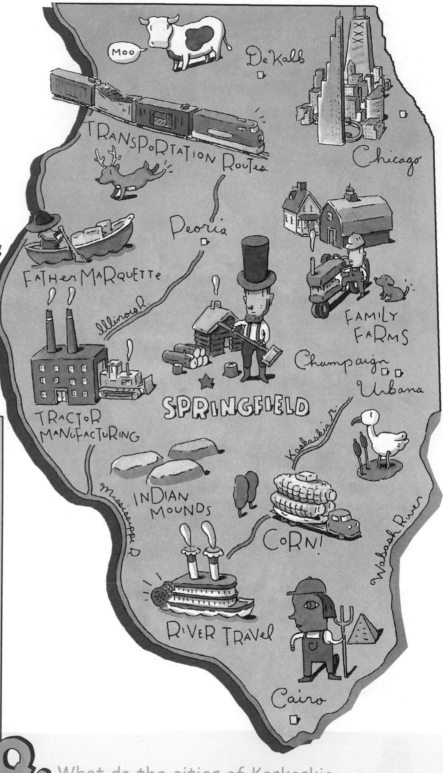

Q. What do the cities of Kaskaskia, Vandalia, and Springfield have in common?

Illinois is in the middle of the country—how did it get so populated?

The rivers! Rivers are very important to Illinois. They're what brought so many Native Americans here long ago, and the French explorers after them. Before cars or planes, the easiest way to move long distances was by water. The Mississippi River was like a giant highway, with lots of other rivers serving as roads. Even today, Illinois's boundaries are largely set by the Mississippi, Ohio, and Wabash rivers.

Who were the explorers you mentioned?

A Frenchman, Father Jacques Marquette, came up the Mississippi back in the 1600s. He and Louis Jolliet were the first Europeans in Illinois. The French built forts and trading posts all along the river, to trap and trade fur.

A. They have all, at one time, been the capital of Illinois.

Life on the prairie back in the day was tough, J.P., but the hard-working farmers prevailed. Today, 80 percent of the state is covered by farms.

Is that why Illinois is called "the Garden Spot of the Nation?"

That's right. Most of Illinois is like a flat tabletop with a patchwork of farms. About one million people work on more than seventy thousand farms or for companies that process Illinois farm products. We export more farm products than any other state. Corn is the most important Illinois crop. Each year Illinois farmers grow about 200 billion ears of corn; we grow more soybeans and raise more hogs than any other state except Iowa. Other farms grow wheat, alfalfa, hay, fruit, and vegetables, or raise cattle, sheep, and chickens.

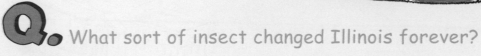

Q. What sort of insect changed Illinois forever?

Illinois is called "the Land of Lincoln," but Abraham Lincoln wasn't even born here.

But this is where he lived as a young man, became a lawyer, and entered politics. He lived in New Salem first, breaking sod to start a farm and trying to make a living in the backwoods. Lincoln wrote that he was raised with an ax in his hand and hardly set it down until he was a man.

As president, Lincoln led the nation through the Civil War. He became known as "the Great Emancipator" for freeing the slaves. But victory came at a terrible price. More than 600,000 Americans were killed in the war, and a few days after the war ended, Lincoln was assassinated.

FOUR SCORE AND SEVEN YEARS AGO*....
* 87 Years

Lincoln was awesome. In his life he worked as a surveyor, a store clerk, a boatman of the Mississippi River, a farmhand, and even postmaster of New Salem!

A. The Caterpillar—but not the insect, the farming machine! Its maker is located in Peoria, and is the world's largest heavy-equipment manufacturer.

At last—Chicago!

I think the famous Illinois poet, Carl Sandburg, said it best:

"HOG Butcher for the World,

Tool Maker, Stacker of Wheat,

Player with Railroads and the Nation's Freight Handler;

Stormy, husky, brawling,

City of the Big Shoulders . . ."

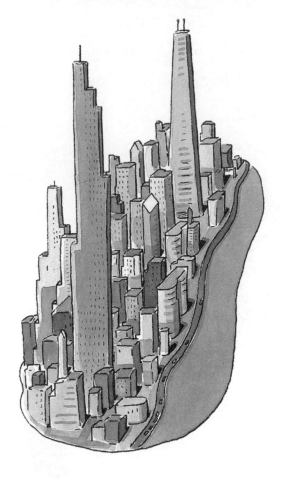

Sandburg used to be a reporter in Chicago, and he saw it at its gutsiest. It started out as a remote trading post in 1779—even in 1830, there were only fifty people here. But then it began to grow fast; it was muddy and filthy, with lots of cheaply built wooden buildings. Disaster struck on October 8, 1871: legend has it Mrs. Catherine O'Leary's cow kicked over a lantern, ignited some hay, and burned down much of Chicago. Twenty thousand buildings were destroyed, 300 people killed, and nearly 100,000 made homeless. But Chicagoans can't be stopped: they rebuilt a beautiful city that today has 3 million residents!

From the farmers to Lincoln to Chicago—it seems like these folks know a little bit about American ingenuity, Lorraine!

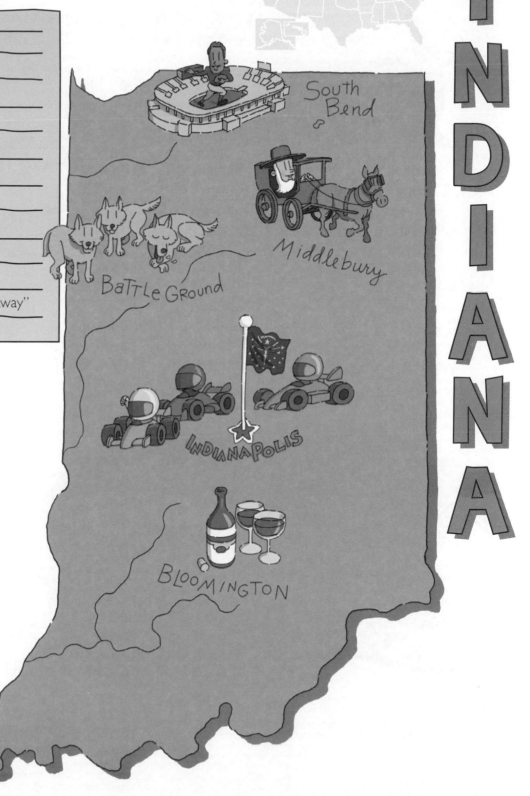

INDIANA

State Capital:	Indianapolis
State Bird:	Cardinal
State Flower:	Peony
State Tree:	Tulip Tree
State Beverage:	Water
State Pie:	Sugar Cream Pie
State Poem:	"Indiana"
State Stone:	Limestone
State Nickname:	Hoosier State ·
State Motto:	"The Crossroads of America"
State Song:	"On the Banks of the Wabash, Far Away"

Indiana became the 19th state in the United States on December 11, 1816. After the Civil War, Indiana became an industrial state, taking an early interest in unions and the suffragist movement, which is equal rights for women.

South Bend

Middlebury

BaTTLe GRound

INDIANAPOLIS

BLOOMINGTON

Anita, they call people from Indiana Hoosiers—why?

No one's really sure, but it might come from a word people used to mean "woods-men," or people that live in the hills. Indiana University teams are called Hoo-siers, too.

I know one thing: Indianapolis is the capital of Indiana, and it's the home of the Indianapolis 500. "Gentlemen, start your engines!"

Oh, you mean the big car race.

It's one of the most important motor racing events in the world—they've been doing it since 1911! Half a million people come to see the Indy 500.

And Indianapolis is called "the Crossroads of the World" because there are so many interstate highways here.

And here's another travel nickname: a house in Fountain City was known as the "Grand Central of the Underground Railroad." It was owned by Levi and Catherine Coffin, and they helped approxi-mately two thousand slaves escape from the South to Canada, in secret, in the years before Abraham Lincoln's Emancipation Proclamation. They had a wagon that was built to hide people,

Q. Is the Indy 500 the only important automobile factor in Indiana?

a secret room in their house, even an extra well so no one would get suspicious at how much water they used.

I know President Lincoln was born in Kentucky and ran for office in Illinois, but I think he grew up here, didn't he?

Yes, he did—the log cabin we always hear about him living in is here in Spencer County. But the one president born in Indiana was William Henry Harrison . . . he was only president for thirty-two days in 1841 before he died in office. He had been a hero in the War of 1812 and governor of the new Indiana Territory.

What's that funny word . . . Tippecanoe? Didn't President Harrison have something to do with the Battle of Tippecanoe?

Hey, you were paying attention in history class! The Native American tribes, led by Tecumseh and his brother, wanted to regain land they had sold to the United States. Harrison was governor of the Indiana Territory then and wanted to expand. When he won the Battle of Tippecanoe, he was a huge hero.

You might notice there are lots of buildings here built out of the same, light beautiful stone.

Is it limestone?

Yes, and Indiana is famous for it—it's the best in the country. The Empire State Building, the Pentagon, even Yankee Stadium are built from it. Especially after the Great Chicago Fire in 1871, many public buildings and colleges in the Midwest started using limestone.

A. No! The state's economy is greatly helped by building auto parts and components. At the start of the twentieth century, classic cars like Duesenbergs, Auburns, Stutzes, and Maxwells were built here.

You know, John Chapman spent a lot of time in these parts.

Who?

Johnny Appleseed! We picture him as a guy traveling around barefoot with a sack full of seeds, but in real life he had a business plan: all over the Midwest he planted saplings and left little nurseries in someone's care. He'd come back and accept money or barter clothes and food for the apple trees. He was a sort of missionary, too, spreading the word of God as he stayed as a guest in countless peoples' homes. He's buried here in Fort Wayne.

I know something about some other Indiana heroes I'll bet you don't know. Name three of the greatest guys ever who were coaches in the Hoosier State.

You think I don't know the answer because I'm a girl? Larry Bird of the Indian Pacers, Knute Rockne of Notre Dame, and Bob Knight of Indian University.

Q. What popular family rock group was from Gary, Indiana?

A. The Jackson 5, whose youngest member was Michael Jackson, "the King of Pop." They started performing in the 1960s, when Michael was just six.

The first American settlers moved to Iowa in 1833. Thirteen years later, on December 28, 1846, Iowa became the 29th state.

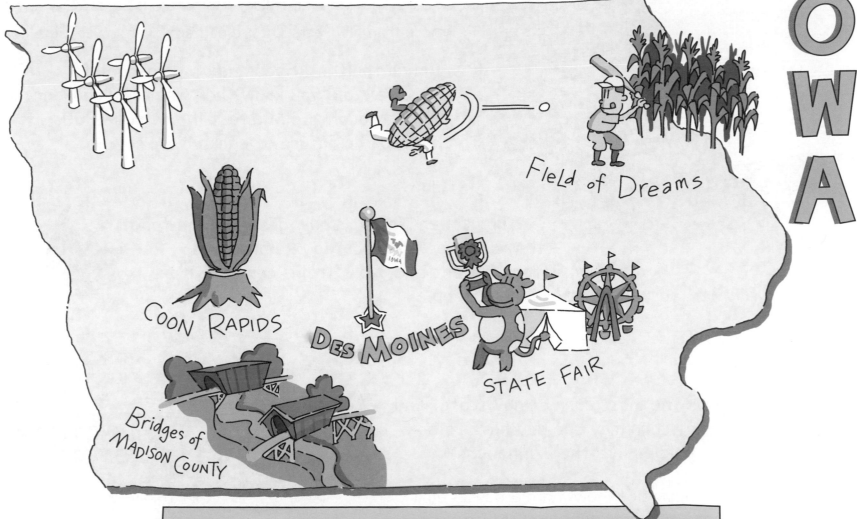

IOWA

Field of Dreams

COON RAPIDS

DES MOINES

STATE FAIR

Bridges of MADISON COUNTY

State Capital:	Des Moines
Major Industries:	agriculture (corn, soybeans, hogs, pigs), food manufacturing, insurance
State Bird:	eastern goldfinch
State Flower:	wild rose
State Tree:	oak
State Nickname:	Hawkeye State
State Motto:	"Our liberties we prize and our rights we will maintain"
State Song:	"The Song of Iowa"

I have a great idea for our road trip around Iowa, Meredith—let's get a Winnebago!

You mean one of those motor homes, Tex?

Sure. They've been making them here is Forest City for more than fifty years. They're named for an Indian tribe.

I'm all for that! Speaking of transportation, Tex, did you know that when the railroad came through the Midwest in the mid-1800s, it changed the future of agriculture?

How?

Back then, farmers only grew enough food that could be transported by horse and wagon before it went bad. Now, trains can take more food farther, faster, and feed more people.

That makes sense. I see loads of cornfields—is growing corn big business here?

Iowa grows the most corn of any state. And guess what corn may one day have to do with vehicles like the Winnebago?

Ummm, wait, I know! Corn produces ethanol!

Q. Which U.S. president was born in West Branch, Iowa?

Right! Henry Ford used ethanol for fuel as far back as the Model T; some rockets have even been fueled by it.

I wonder if it can fuel an elevator. The Fenelon Place Elevator in Dubuque, Iowa's oldest city, is also a sort of train called a funicular. They say it's the shortest and steepest in the world: the ride is only 296 feet long. The man who built it worked at the bottom of the hill, and it took too long to walk back up for lunch, so he devised this train!

Let's take a ride!

Some cool stuff goes on here in Iowa. There's a weeklong bike ride called RAGBRAI that goes across the whole state—472 miles! It started in 1972, when two reporters thought they'd try to do the ride and write stories for the newspaper along the way. They asked the public to join them, and to their surprise, 300 people showed up. Now they have to put a limit on it because it's so popular: 8,500 riders.

Here's the best part: everyone dips their back bike wheel in the Missouri River at the start, and when they get to the finish, their front wheel goes in the Mississippi River.

I know why they do that! Iowa is the only state whose east and west borders are natural ones: the Missouri and Mississippi rivers.

A. Herbert Clark Hoover (1874–1964) was the first president to be born west of the Mississippi River, and one of only two presidents to be elected without having held a previous electoral office. He also wrote more than a dozen books!

Since your name is Tex, I'll bet you know that probably the greatest movie cowboy who ever lived, grew up in Winterset. His name was Marion Mitchell Morrison.

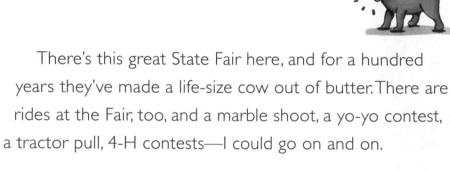

A guy named Marion? I've never heard of that.

It was John Wayne's real name! He was in more than one hundred movies, and not just as a cowboy. You'll see him in a lot of war movies, too. He was one of the *best* movie stars ever.

OK, there's one thing I've got to see before we leave Iowa: the butter cow.

What the heck . . . ?

PIE EATING CONTEST

There's this great State Fair here, and for a hundred years they've made a life-size cow out of butter. There are rides at the Fair, too, and a marble shoot, a yo-yo contest, a tractor pull, 4-H contests—I could go on and on.

I'll bet there's even a pie-eating contest. I'm in! Nothing says America like a state fair!

Q. What is odd about Iowa's spelling?

A. It's the only state that starts with two vowels. The name comes from the Ioway people, an Indian tribe in the area when Europeans started exploring in the 1600s.

State Capital:	Topeka
State Bird:	Western Meadowlark
State Flower:	Wild Native Sunflower
State Tree:	Cottonwood
State Animal:	American Buffalo
Sate Amphibian:	Barred Tiger Salamander
State Reptile:	Ornate Box Turtle
State Insect:	Honeybee
State March:	"The Kansas March"
State Nickname:	Sunflower State
State Motto:	"Ad astra per aspera" ("To the stars through difficulties")

KANSAS

Kansas became our 34th state on January 29, 1861. It is on the Kansas River, and both were named after the Kansa Indians.

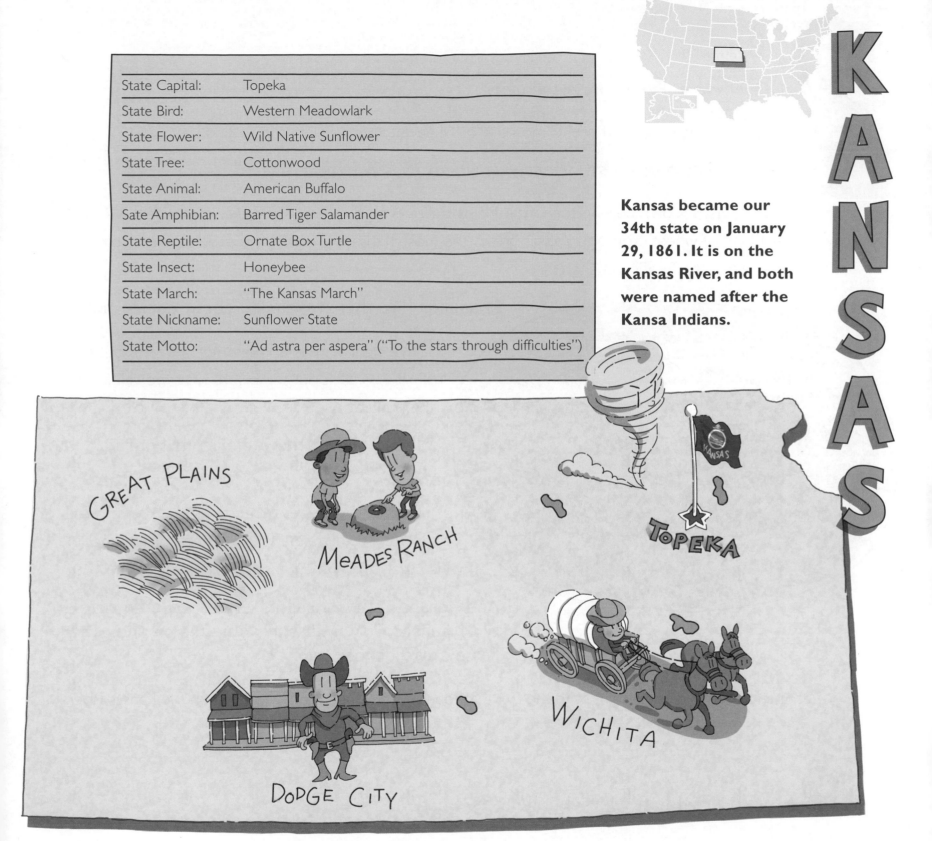

GREAT PLAINS

MEADES RANCH

TOPEKA

DODGE CITY

WICHITA

Beau, where are you?

Over here, Penny, in the wheat.

There's wheat everywhere! C'mon out or I'll have to send Skipper in to find you.

Phew, I almost got lost. There was wheat everywhere I turned.

Lots of it's grown here in the Great Plains states. A type called hard red winter wheat is America's largest kind of wheat crop, and Kansas grows the most. Kansans grow the most sunflowers, too—its nickname is even "the Sunflower State."

It sounds like this state is all about agriculture.

You're right, Kansas is known for growing, but originally it was all about the bison, or as we call it now, the buffalo.

I'll bet the Native Americans hunted them here.

Yup. Lots of tribes hunted in these parts. In fact, this state was named after the Kanza, or Kaw people, which is also how the Kansas River got its name.

And Kansas *City*, Kansas, is what's called a satellite city of Kansas City, Missouri, which is on the other side of the state border, right?

Yes, that can be confusing, along with the fact that Topeka is the state capital, which is on the Kansas River!

Q. What president grew up in Kansas?

Kanza means "people of the wind." No wonder Dodge City is the windiest city in the country.

Isn't that where all the heroes were lawmen—guys like Bat Masterson, "Wild Bill" Hickok, and Wyatt Earp?

They were keeping the gunslingers and cowboys in line back in the 1800s. That's also the time where Kansas's state song was written.

I know that one: "Home on the Range"! It even starts out, "Oh, give me a home, where the buffalo roam . . ."

". . . and the deer and the antelope play."

A. Dwight D. Eisenhower (1890–1969) spent his childhood in Abilene. Our thirty-fourth president was a five-star general who put America in the space race, built our modern highway system, and stopped the Korean War.

When we were talking about weather, we didn't mention that Kansas is located in what weathermen call Tornado Alley, did we Penny—or should I say, *Dorothy*!

You're making a *Wizard of Oz* joke, aren't you?

Ha! Yes, I am. Dorothy was living in Kansas when that giant tornado came and *whoosh!* It knocked her right on her head.

And remember, she says, "Toto, I don't think we're in Kansas anymore!"

When I look at a map, Kansas looks like it's right in the middle of the country, doesn't it?

DEAD CENTER

Meades Ranch

KANSAS

UNITED STATES

It's funny you say that . . . because it is! Welcome to Meades Ranch, which is the center of what's called the contiguous United States—that means the states on the North American continent, so that doesn't include Alaska and Hawaii. What's totally cool is that when you see surveyors with their

Q. What is a prairie chicken?

78

equipment, they are checking and measuring everything in relationship to where we're standing right now.

Every surveyor in the—what is it?—contiguous United States?

Yes, sir! Isn't that amazing?

You know what woman was really cool, besides Dorothy, who also came from Kansas? Amelia Earhart.

I love her, too! She was so brave. They call her an aviatrix—men are called aviators. She was the first woman to fly solo across the Atlantic Ocean. She was all for women's rights, too. She disappeared in flight, though, which was so sad.

It doesn't make her any less heroic, though. I think maybe she was even more awesome than Dorothy.

 A. It's not actually a chicken, and Kansas has the largest population in North America. It looks a little like a hen, or a turkey, or a rooster, but it's actually a wild grouse!

79

KENTUCKY

LOUISVILLE

FRANKFORT

CUMBERLAND GAP

FORT KNOX

Mammoth Cave

LINCOLN'S LOG CABIN

No major Native American tribes ever laid claim to Kentucky, though they had hunted here since about 1000 BC. During the Civil War, some Kentuckians signed an Order of Secession to become part of Jefferson Davis's Confederacy, though officially Kentucky was known as a border state, along with Delaware, Maryland, Missouri, and West Virginia.

The first Kentucky Fried Chicken—or KFC—was served in 1930 by Colonel Sanders himself at a gas station he owned in North Corbin, Kentucky. It was finger-lickin' good!

State Nickname:	the Bluegrass State
State Capital:	Frankfort
Date Entered the Union:	June 1, 1792
State Motto:	"United we stand, divided we fall"
State Flower:	goldenrod
State Bird:	Kentucky cardinal
State Song:	"My Old Kentucky Home"
State Tree:	tulip poplar
State Mammal:	thoroughbred horse
State Fish:	Kentucky (spotted) bass

Q. What rare natural phenomenon occurs at Kentucky's Cumberland Falls?

Hey, I know a little bit about Louisville. It's Kentucky's biggest city.

That's where they have the Kentucky Derby, that big horse race.

The biggest. It doesn't last very long, but they call it "the most exciting two minutes in sports." It started way back in 1875. Everyone gets really dressed up and the ladies wear these awesome hats. We can also go to "Thunder over Louisville," the fireworks display that's part of the Derby celebration. It's the biggest in the whole country.

You know Kentucky is called "the Bluegrass State," right, because of the special grass they grow here? It's used everywhere for parks and lawns—and the horses love it, too. But then there's also bluegrass *music*. It's a little like country music, but sounds sort of like jazz and the blues, too. Scottish and Irish immigrants, like your family, and African Americans, like mine, created it. There's a lot of fiddling!

My dad told me about bluegrass music. I'd love to hear some.

A. A moonbow! Also sometimes called a lunar rainbow, it's produced by light that's reflected off the moon's surface, not from direct sunlight like a rainbow.

I've heard about another cool thing to see here: Mammoth Cave National Park. It's the longest cave system in the world. They've been doing tours here for two hundred years.

Wow! Some of the tours are six hours and go for five miles. And there are some sort of extreme tours where you crawl in the mud and go through tunnels.

Yuk. You go—I'm going to a bluegrass music festival.

You know, we learn so much about Abraham Lincoln living in Illinois, but he was born right here in Kentucky.

In a log cabin, right?

Yup. And he was the first president born in the west. But someone else was born here, too, who called himself president: Jefferson Davis.

Who was he?

He was president of the Confederate States of America during the American Civil War—the same time that Lincoln was president of the United States. He grew up less than 100 miles from here.

OK, that's just weird.

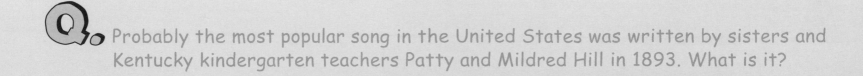

Q. Probably the most popular song in the United States was written by sisters and Kentucky kindergarten teachers Patty and Mildred Hill in 1893. What is it?

One of my heroes is from this state, too. I'll bet you don't know who Muhammad Ali is.

Are you kidding? Only the best heavyweight champion of all time! He used to say that he could "float like a butterfly and sting like a bee."

You're right! Even *he* called himself "the Greatest"!

Hey, George, isn't Fort Knox near here?

Right again, Mimi, although its real name is the United States Bullion Depository, built near Fort Knox, Kentucky. It holds more than 4,600 tons of gold. And before you ask, no, they don't give out samples!

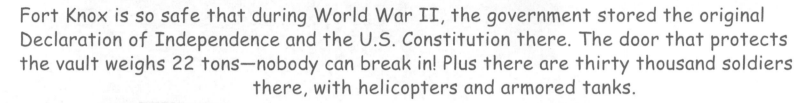

Fort Knox is so safe that during World War II, the government stored the original Declaration of Independence and the U.S. Constitution there. The door that protects the vault weighs 22 tons—nobody can break in! Plus there are thirty thousand soldiers there, with helicopters and armored tanks.

Aside from guarding gold, I wonder what other kind of work people do around here.

I know that coal mining is one of the largest industries—they call coal the "black diamond" because it's so valuable. It's still the biggest source of energy for electricity in the whole world.

A. "Happy Birthday to You," of course. There's a man who claims he bought the copyright to the song, which means he thinks he should be paid every time someone sings it!

LOUISIANA

State Bird

Natchitoches

BATON ROUGE

New Orleans

Louisiana was named after Louis XIV of France by explorer Robert La Salle. He explored much of the Mississippi River and the Gulf of Mexico. It became the 18th state in 1812.

Nickname:	Pelican State or Sportsman's Paradise
Date Entered the Union:	April 30, 1812, the eighteenth state
State Fossil:	petrified palmwood
State Motto:	"Union, Justice and Confidence"
State Songs:	"Give Me Louisiana" and "You Are My Sunshine"
State Bird:	eastern brown pelican
State Flower:	magnolia
State Tree:	bald cypress
State Dog:	Catahoula leopard dog
Products:	agricultural sugarcane, strawberries, sweet potatoes, rice, cotton, corn, potatoes, soybeans, citrus fruits, pecans, perique tobacco, aquaculture lumber, mineral petroleum, natural gas, salt, sulfur, carbon black, gravel

Louisiana is the only state that is not divided into counties; it is broken down by what is called parishes.

Q. What are cracklings?

Becky, remind me about the Louisiana Purchase again. History isn't my best subject!

In 1803, Thomas Jefferson actually bought this gigantic piece of land from France. He wanted to be sure that France or Spain didn't block our access to New Orleans, an important port in the Gulf of Mexico. If you look at a map, you'll see it was bigger than the thirteen original colonies! The Louisiana Purchase included part of what are now fourteen states and two Canadian provinces.

You're right—it was humongous!

Even now, when you go to parts of Louisiana, it almost feels like another country. Do you know about Cajun people, music, or food?

No . . .

They live here, but are mostly descendants of people from parts of Canada that speak French, so they talk in a sort of half-English, half-French language that's called a dialect. Their music, which has lots of accordion, is called Cajun or Zydecko. And the food—yum! Cajun food is often made with local things like rabbit or crayfish, and vegetables and grains like rice and okra.

Ao Other places they're called pork rinds. They are a snack made of fried pigskins!

What's a crayfish? I've heard about them.

They look like tiny little lobsters. Let's go to a crayfish boil! They're served with sausage, potatoes and corn-on-the-cob: it's my favorite meal ever, and you hardly get it anywhere else in the country. Ninety-eight percent of the little critters come from Louisiana, and almost three-quarters of them never leave the state because they're so delicious!

Where do you find them?

Louisiana has a lot of bayous, which are slow-moving rivers. That's where crayfish live, and the shrimp, too.

Not everything interesting is out on the bayou. Baton Rouge is the capital, I know that. But isn't the biggest city New Orleans?

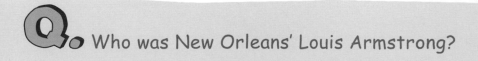

Who was New Orleans' Louis Armstrong?

Yes, and one of the most awesome cities anywhere. For one thing, it's home to incredibly brave people, who are determined to rebuild after the city was devastated by Hurricane Katrina. And it's also the home of Mardi Gras!

Is that more French?

Yes, it means "Fat Tuesday." That's because Mardi Gras always starts on Ash Wednesday, the first day of Lent for Roman Catholics. In the old days, people used to fast and give up their favorite foods for the forty days of Lent. So they'd celebrate big time on Fat Tuesday.

Mardi Gras has sure gotten to be a huge celebration. How about these crazy parades?

They go on for days now and in cities all over the world, but New Orleans is the real home of Mardi Gras. Let's put on some costumes and go to the parade tonight. They throw beads off the floats and we can catch some!

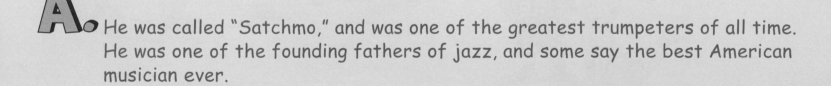

A. He was called "Satchmo," and was one of the greatest trumpeters of all time. He was one of the founding fathers of jazz, and some say the best American musician ever.

Whoa! Check out that long bridge! I can't even see the other end.

That's called the Lake Pontchartrain Causeway. It is the longest bridge in the entire world that goes completely over water. It starts in Metarie, right next to New Orleans, and goes to Mandeville. It's almost 24 miles long.

Hey, I do know one piece of history from around here. Remember the Battle of New Orleans?

Sort of . . .

Andrew Jackson, before he was president, was a general and he led the battle. It went on for two weeks. What he didn't know was that the whole War of 1812 was declared over the day after the Battle of New Orleans started.

Yipes. I guess that's what happens when you don't have a cell phone.

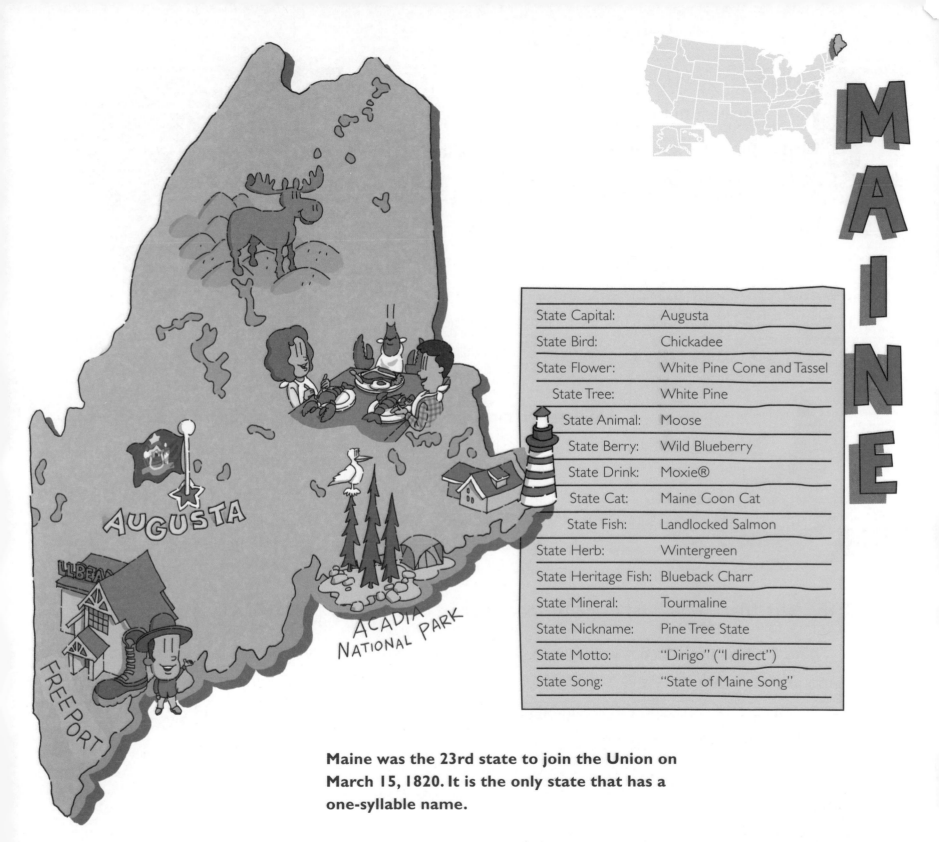

State Capital:	Augusta
State Bird:	Chickadee
State Flower:	White Pine Cone and Tassel
State Tree:	White Pine
State Animal:	Moose
State Berry:	Wild Blueberry
State Drink:	Moxie®
State Cat:	Maine Coon Cat
State Fish:	Landlocked Salmon
State Herb:	Wintergreen
State Heritage Fish:	Blueback Charr
State Mineral:	Tourmaline
State Nickname:	Pine Tree State
State Motto:	"Dirigo" ("I direct")
State Song:	"State of Maine Song"

Maine was the 23rd state to join the Union on March 15, 1820. It is the only state that has a one-syllable name.

Hey Rick, have you ever heard of the Appalachian Trail?

Sure. My dad says that one of these days he's going to hike the whole thing. He makes it sound like it's really long.

Long? I guess! It's 2,178 miles! It starts way down in Georgia, and comes all the way up here, to Maine in New England. It can take months to do the whole thing, but you can jump on anywhere and walk a little bit.

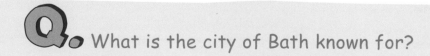

He'll never make it. But I'll bet my dog Skipper could.

Maybe he'd just rather come see the easternmost point in the United States. Funnily enough, it's called West Quoddy, right here in Maine. Let's get our sleeping bags: if we wake up here at the lighthouse, we'll be the first people in the whole United States to see the sun come up.

I thought there would be more beaches here—the coast is pretty rocky.

There are beaches, too, but you're right. It is not a welcoming coast. Even before the Pilgrims came to Plymouth, Massachusetts, the British tried to settle in Maine in the Popham Colony in 1607. The climate was pretty nasty and the Indian attacks didn't help, either. The settlers didn't last long and went back to England.

Q. What is the city of Bath known for?

I know one good thing that comes from Maine's rocky coast: lobsters! Yum!

Lots of lobsters. Like over 90% of the lobsters people eat in the entire United States come from here.

And blueberries!

Yup— we grow more blueberries than anywhere else in the world!

Maine seems like lots of fun—do you go skiing a lot?

Sure. Downhill skiing and cross-country, too. Not only is it fun but tourism is big business in Maine. There's lots of deer, moose and bear hunting, camping, sport fishing, snowmobiling, and of course sailing. My dad helps run a ski resort.

Wow. I think I'll get a job here when I grow up.

Augusta is our capital, but I love living in Portland. Some people come here just for the great restaurants. It's also a really popular small city to start a business. Maybe you'll grow up to be an entrepreneur. Maybe we'll go into business together!

A. Maine has been building ships for more than 400 years. The Bath Iron Works has built all kinds of boats, and in World War II it built one destroyer every 17 days.

I know there's a beautiful National Park here, too, called Acadia.

That's right, Rick. It covers a lot of beautiful Mount Desert Island, with lakes, mountains, and oceans, all in one place. Another place we could bring our sleeping bags! That is, if the Bass Harbor Head Light House doesn't keep us awake.

I swear there's a lighthouse everywhere I look. How many do you think there are in Maine?

I know that answer—71!

Carla, what is that weird pile of shells? It's taller than my house, I'll bet!

This is called the Whaleback Shell Midden. It's just what you think it is—a gigantic heap of shells. Places like this built up over the centuries near the shore or at mouths of rivers. Prehistoric people ate shellfish and dumped the shells here. Sometimes you find ceramics, bones, and tools, too.

Wow, that's a lot of oyster dinners! Maine is cool, especially if you like history, like I do.

Q. What is Maine's nickname?

A. "The Pine Tree State." In fact, the nation's first sawmill was established near York, Maine in 1623.

Maryland is a mid-Atlantic state that entered the Union as the 7th state on April 28, 1788. It is often classified as a Southern state as it falls below the Mason-Dixon Line, but it was a "border state" during the Civil War. Soldiers from those states who were brothers often fought on opposite sides.

The American flag flies over "The Star-Spangled Banner" composer Francis Scott Key's grave in Frederick, Maryland, twenty-four hours a day. Fewer than ten places in the United States are allowed to fly the flag after sundown.

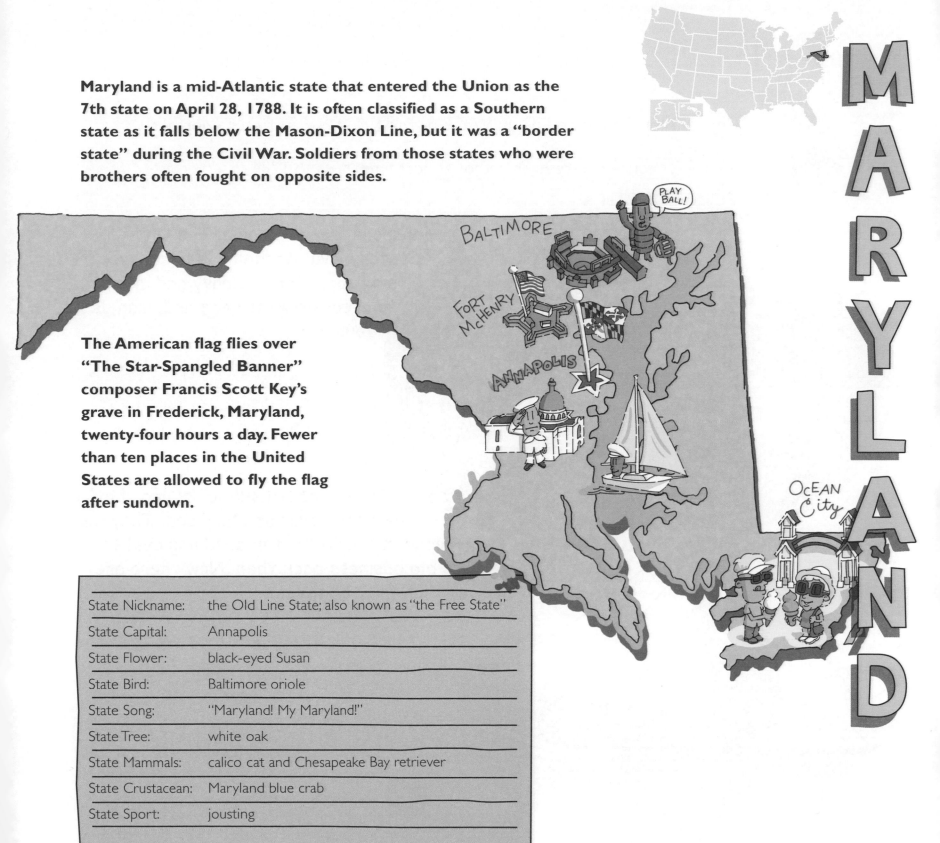

State Nickname:	the Old Line State; also known as "the Free State"
State Capital:	Annapolis
State Flower:	black-eyed Susan
State Bird:	Baltimore oriole
State Song:	"Maryland! My Maryland!"
State Tree:	white oak
State Mammals:	calico cat and Chesapeake Bay retriever
State Crustacean:	Maryland blue crab
State Sport:	jousting

Here we are in Annapolis, Maryland's capital. Remember when it was the capital of the United States?

What?! No! Everyone knows Washington DC is our nation's capital.

Gotcha! Of course you're right, but for a short time, 1783 to 1784, it served as our temporary capital.

Annapolis is so awesome. The United States Naval Academy is here, preparing people for the navy and marines. My cousin went here and, man, is it tough!

It looks it! They're so lucky to be here on the Chesapeake Bay, though—it's beautiful. But Josh, do you know the name of those weird boats?

They're called skipjacks and they're the State Boat of Maryland. They were made in the 1800s for dredging oysters, which was big business back then. Now there are fewer than fifty of them.

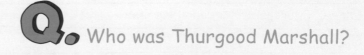 **Q.** Who was Thurgood Marshall?

Let's see if someone will take us sailing on one. Did you know the Chesapeake Bay is actually an estuary?

Hmmm, let me try to remember the definition from school: an estuary is a "partly enclosed coastal body of water with one or more rivers or streams flowing into it, and with a free connection to the open sea." Am I right?

A+! This is the largest one in the whole country. And it gives us all those delicious crabs.

Yummmm. Soft-shelled crabs and blue crabs, with their crazy claws. They're my favorite part about Maryland.

Baltimore's a fun place, too. People often think it's the capital of Maryland—it's more than six times larger than the next-biggest city. I want to take you to my favorite place here, the B&O Railroad Museum.

Wow! It's even at a railroad station.

Not just any railroad station: this is the Mount Clare station, and they call it the birthplace of American railroading. The first regular passenger service started from right where we're standing, back in 1830. It went to Ellicott City, which is not even a thirteen-mile trip!

A. He was the Baltimore native who was the first African American to serve on the United Sates Supreme Court in 1967. He was the winning lawyer in a 1954 case called *Brown v. Board of Education*, which integrated black and white kids in public schools.

Hey, look at this—this brochure says that this is also where Morse code began.

I know! The first Morse code message was sent from here by Samuel F. B. Morse himself to the Capitol Building in Washington DC. Morse was originally a painter, but stopped when his wife died and no one could reach him in time to tell him to come home. He dedicated himself to improving long-distance communications.

Gee, today most people can't even live five minutes without their cell phones.

Well, I'll tell you about something incredible that's been here way before cell phones *or* Samuel Morse: the wild horses of Assateague.

What makes them wild?

No one's sure: some say a Spanish galleon shipwrecked and the horses on the ship swam to Assateaugue Island. More likely, colonists left them on the island to avoid a tax on fenced livestock. Wild horses have been here since the 1600s! Every summer they swim across a channel to another island called Chincoteague. Some are bought by people at an auction there and become tamed.

Q. What was the Battle of Antietam?

A. In 1862, it was the first big battle of the Civil War to take place on what was considered Northern soil. To this day, it remains the deadliest one-day battle in our history. More than twenty-three thousand soldiers were killed.

Massachusetts became the 6th state in the USA on February 6, 1788. Throughout its history, it has been known for its political families, like the Adamses, the Lodges, and the Kennedys.

There is a house in Rockport built entirely of newspaper.

State Capital:	Boston
State Bird:	chickadee
State Flower:	mayflower
State Tree:	American elm
State Cat:	tabby cat
State Dog:	Boston terrier
State Fish:	cod
State Game Bird:	wild turkey
State Artist:	Norman Rockwell
State Bean:	baked navy bean
State Berry:	cranberry
State Beverage:	cranberry juice

State Children's Book:	"Make Way for Ducklings"
State Dessert:	Boston cream pie
State Historical Rock:	Plymouth Rock
State Mammal:	right whale
State Poem:	"Blue Hills of Massachusetts"
State Shell:	New England Neptune
State Nickname:	Bay State
State Motto:	"Ense petit placidam sub libertate quietem" (By the sword we seek peace, but peace only under liberty)
State Song:	"All Hail to Massachusetts"

MASSACHUSETTS

Here we are, J.P., at the very tippity-tip of Cape Cod, Provincetown.

Wow! I could have sworn I just saw a whale!

You did—that was the tail, or fluke, of a right whale.

Are there wrong whales, Lorraine?

They were named right whale because whalers considered them the "right" whales to hunt. They were rich in blubber, making them slow swimmers, so they were easy to catch.

Wait, I thought whales were endangered and you couldn't kill them.

That's true now, but back before oil was discovered in the ground, people used oil from whale blubber as fuel to light their homes. The most valuable whale oil is called spermaceti and is from the whale's brain. It was used in watches and other fine machinery.

I know New Bedford was the whaling capital of the world. The novel *Moby-Dick* starts out in New Bedford.

You're right. In the mid-1800s, whaling made it the richest city in America.

Didn't the Pilgrims land around here?

They landed in Plymouth, after sailing from England on the *Mayflower* in 1620. In fact, they first stopped in Provincetown for five weeks, where the future colonists made the Mayflower Compact. All the men signed the

Q. Where is the oldest graffiti in North America?

250-word statement declaring that they would "combine ourselves into a Civil Body Politick for our better Ordering and Preservation." They soon selected William Bradford as their leader. It was the start of American democracy.

Whoa! Plymouth looks just like it did almost four hundred years ago!

Ha! This is Plimoth Plantation, the living history museum of the Pilgrim village in 1627. The first year was horrible for the Pilgrims. They were cold, hungry, and only about half of them made it through the winter. It was a Pawtuxet Indian named Squanto that helped the remaining people through.

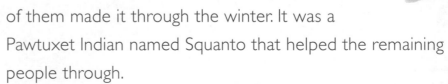

He said "Hello"

How?

He served as a translator for the new colonists, and showed them how to hunt and trap, and which crops to grow. The first harvest was celebrated in the fall of 1621.

The first Thanksgiving!

A. Colonists found a rock in Berkley, Massachusetts, covered with writings, pictures, dates, and other markings. Nobody knows if it was Native Americans, Vikings, or other colonists who did the writing.

I'll bet you've heard about the Salem witch trials, too.

Just a little bit.

Puritans accused different men and women of being agents of the devil. The most famous witch hunt took place in Salem in 1692, when at least 150 people—including children—were arrested and 19 were hanged. The accusations got so ridiculous that the governor finally stopped the trials, but the town and its people were torn apart.

Are we near Boston?

Yup! Boston became the capital of the Massachusetts Bay Company in 1630, when one thousand Puritans arrived. They elected John Winthrop as their first governor. He promised the colonists they would create a "city on the hill" that would serve as a version of heaven on earth. I think it still is. Go, Red Sox!

I know you're a Red Sox fan, but wasn't basketball actually invented in Massachusetts?

Sure was! At a YMCA in Springfield, a teacher placed two peach baskets at each end of a local gym as an experiment for a new game. It was an instant hit!

Q. What was the "Curse of the Bambino?"

Hey, wasn't Dr. Seuss from Springfield?

He sure was. This is also the home of the Springfield rifle; half of all the weapons carried by Union soldiers during the Civil War were made here. Lots of other famous writers came from Massachusetts: Henry David Thoreau, Ralph Waldo Emerson—my favorite is Emily Dickinson. She lived in her family's house and hardly ever left it; only a couple of her poems were published when she was alive. But after she died, her poetry was discovered and she has become of the world's favorite poets.

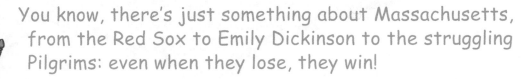

You know, there's just something about Massachusetts, from the Red Sox to Emily Dickinson to the struggling Pilgrims: even when they lose, they win!

A. In 1920, the Boston Red Sox traded baseball great Babe Ruth—known as "the Bambino"—to the New York Yankees for $125,000. Some think that's why it took eighty-four years for the Red Sox to win the World Series again!

MICHIGAN

Michigan was the 26th state admitted to the Union on January 26, 1837.

The name "Michigan" is a French adaptation of the Ojibwe Indian word for "large water," *mishigama.*

State Capital:	Lansing
Largest City:	Detroit
State Bird:	robin
State Flower:	apple blossom
State Wildflower:	dwarf lake iris
State Mammal:	white-tailed deer
State Tree:	white pine
State Reptile:	painted turtle
State Nickname:	Wolverine State
State Motto:	"Si quaeris peninsulam amoenam, circum spice" (If you are seeking a pleasant peninsula, look around you)
State Song:	"Michigan, My Michigan"

Harry Blackstone Sr., one of the world's most famous magicians, called the tiny town of Colon "the Magic Capital of the World." He is buried here and a four-day magic convention in Colon annually doubles the population of that one thousand-person hamlet.

Q. What are you never more than 6 miles away from in Michigan?

OSSINEKE
Dinosaur Garden

MANISTEE

BATTLE CREEK

LANSING

DETROIT

Allen Park

The Mitten State!

What? That's not Michigan's nickname.

Maybe not, but it's shaped like a mitten.

You're right! At least some of it is—what about that whole part to the west?

That's called the Upper Peninsula—the mitten is the Lower; Michigan is the only state made up entirely of two peninsulas. Right between the two of them are the Straits of Mackinac; they're only 5 miles wide, and connect two of the Great Lakes, Michigan and Huron. Right between them is Mackinac Island. I'll take you there.

What's so great about it? It's not very big.

I know, but it's totally fun. I went with my parents last summer and we stayed at its gigantic Grand Hotel, which was built in 1887 and boasts the world's largest porch.

Hey, Carla, there are no cars here.

Isn't it great? It's bikes and horse-and-carriages. There's a British fort here where you can fire a real cannon, plus sailing, biking, and my favorite . . . fudge eating.

You know what's funny? That Mackinac Island has no cars, and Detroit, right here in Michigan, is the biggest automobile city in the country.

Ha! That's true, Rick.

A. An inland lake—and you're never more than 85 miles from one of the Great Lakes!

It all started in 1899, when Henry Ford built his first car company here. Other companies joined in, but Ford was the king. He began using an assembly line to build cars, which was really innovative. And when building cars became big business, it made Detroit a big city.

I think of one other thing when I think of Detroit: Motown! Berry Gordy started this music company in the 1960s with African-American musicians and brought soul music to the airwaves.

My mom has all of their music: Marvin Gaye, the Supremes, Stevie Wonder!

The "Motown Sound" never gets old!

Are all the Great Lakes near here?

Lake Erie, Huron, Michigan, and Superior are all part of this state's waterfront. The only one that doesn't touch part of Michigan is Lake Ontario. Since Michigan is in the Midwest, it's easy to forget there is so much water around.

Q. Why is Michigan called "the Wolverine State"?

But you know what? I read it has more shoreline than any other state except Alaska.

And get this: Michigan has more light-houses than any other state—150! I would have thought somewhere like California had the most. Michigan is full of surprises.

And here's a good one: what's so weird about the zip code 48222? I'll give you a hint: more water.

Water doesn't have a zip code!

Technically, no, but the floating post office does!

I have to see this!

For over one hundred years, a boat on the Detroit River has been delivering mail to sailors at work on different boats as they pass by. Usually, the big boat drops a bucket overboard and picks up its "mail by the pail." Sometimes there are even special deliveries, like a pizza!

A. Some say their Ohio neighbors, battling with them over a piece of land, said Michigan folks were vicious as wolverines. Funny thing is, there are no wolverines in Michigan!

If it floated down the Huron River, it would want to stop in Ann Arbor. The city's not one of Michigan's biggest, but it is home to the University of Michigan.

Go, Wolverines!

Right! It's a Big Ten Conference school for sports. Research is one of the things UM is known for. For us kids there's a great place where we can sort of do our own research: the Ann Arbor Hands-On Museum.

It's an old firehouse, and there are 250 interactive exhibits. We can play around while learning about geology, math, physics, and music!

When we grow up, I'll work here—you can work on the floating post office!

State Capital:	Saint Paul
State Bird:	common loon
State Flower:	pink and white lady's slipper
State Fruit:	Honeycrisp apple
State Tree:	red pine or Norway pine
State Butterfly:	monarch
State Fish:	walleye pike
State Gemstone:	Lake Superior agate
State Grain:	wild rice
State Muffin:	blueberry
State Mushroom:	morel
State Photograph:	"Grace," by Eric Enstrom
State Song:	"Hail! Minnesota"
State Nickname:	Gopher State, North Star State
State Motto:	"L'Étoile du Nord" (the star of the north)
State Song:	"Hail Minnesota"

Minnesota became our 32nd state on May 11, 1858. Apart from Alaska, it is our northernmost state, and some of the oldest rocks in the world have been found there.

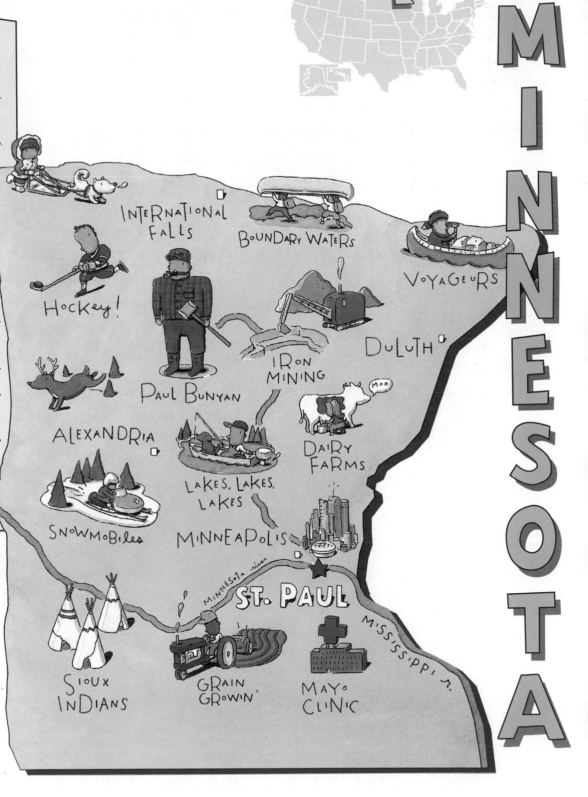

I've heard Minnesota being called "the Land of Ten Thousand Lakes." That can't be true.

It's not. There are more like fifteen thousand! Even the name Minnesota comes from an Indian word meaning "cloud-reflecting water." And we know how to use those lakes—there are more than 2 million boats in the state, nearly one for every two people. *And* Minnesotans introduced waterskiing to the world.

Well, what are the big cities here, Scott—the Twin Cities?

Right, Elsa: Minneapolis and Saint Paul. Almost half the people in the whole state live in this urban area—the two cities are divided by the Mississippi River. Minneapolis is more the financial and cultural city of the two. Saint Paul is 10 miles to the east; it's quieter, with more neighborhoods and fewer big buildings.

And more dogs, Pumpkin!

Now, a little bit about Minnesota's iron mining.

Oh, snore.

Q. Can you guess what winter vehicle was built in Roseau, Minnesota, in 1953?

C'mon, I promise, it's interesting! We're the top iron-mining state. In an area called "the Iron Range," prospectors discovered iron "veins" in the 1880s. One of them was the Mesabi Range: 120 miles long and full of metal. It produced nearly one-third of the *world's* iron supply until the 1950s! Immigrants poured into Minnesota to work in these giant open-pit mines, and at the factories that turned iron into steel. We helped arm the nation during World Wars I and II—you could say we shaped America's history.

You're right. That's cool.

Now how about something quirkier: Paul Bunyan. He is a huge—and I do mean *huge*—Minnesota myth. Legend has it he was a lumberjack who could fell giant trees with a single swipe of his ax. And he has this giant blue ox, Babe. He's a part of the lore of Minnesota logging.

There are statues of him and Babe everywhere.

The biggest one is 33 feet high, outside of the Paul Bunyan History Museum in Akeley. There's even a Paul Bunyan Amusement Center.

A. The slippery slope-defying snowmobile!

If we have time, I think I'd prefer a trip to the Mall of America.

I don't blame you—it's fun! In Bloomington, this megalithic mall is the largest of its kind in the nation, and the number one attraction in Minnesota. It has more than five hundred stores, but that's the least of it. There is a 1.2-million-gallon aquarium, a pirate ship playground, a virtual submarine ride, a theme park—complete with a roller coaster—and a seventy-five-seat Chapel of Love!

Just in case you are at the mall and want to get married! You gotta love Minnesota!

Q. Who is Jesse Ventura?

A. The ex-governor of Minnesota was also a professional wrestler and a Navy Underwater Demolition Teams expert!

State Capital:	Jackson
State Bird:	Mockingbird
State Flower:	Magnolia
State Wildflower:	Coreopsis
State Tree:	Magnolia
State Fossil:	Prehistoric Whale
State Land Mammal:	White-tailed deer Red Fox
State Reptile:	American Alligator
State Shell:	Oyster Shell
State Stone:	Petrified Wood
State Toy:	Teddy Bear
State Waterfowl:	Wood Duck
State Water Mammal:	Bottlenose Dolphin
State Nickname:	Magnolia State
State Motto:	"Virtute et armis" ("By valor and arms")
State Song:	"Go Mis-sis-sip-pi"

Mississippi became our 20th state on December 10, 1817. Though Mississippi was a slave state, there was a class of free people of color.

Peter, what's the first thing you think of when you think of Mississippi?

Well, I think of learning to spell it, of course, and then I think of playing hide-and-seek and saying *one-Mississippi, two-Mississippi* to count because it's such a long word.

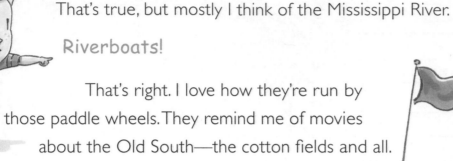

That's true, but mostly I think of the Mississippi River.

Riverboats!

That's right. I love how they're run by those paddle wheels. They remind me of movies about the Old South—the cotton fields and all.

Have they always grown cotton in the South?

Yes, but it was almost destroyed by the boll weevil, a tiny beetle that eats cotton plants. Before that, they used to say, "Cotton is King," because growing cotton is what made many people in this state so rich way back in the 1850s.

Q. What does a teddy bear have to do with Mississippi?

But all the work in the fields was done by slaves while the white plantation owners became wealthy. That was one of the reasons they wanted to secede from the Union during the Civil War: the states in the north wanted to abolish slavery. More than half the people who lived in Mississippi were slaves!

So in a way, it's not so surprising that the civil rights movement in the 1960s really took hold here in Mississippi. The rest of America really got to see what it was like when the Freedom Riders—buses filled with both black and white activists—were arrested and mistreated by police when they got to the state's capital, Jackson.

It was a dark time in American history, that's for sure. Abraham Lincoln may have freed the slaves, but it took another hundred years for President Lyndon B. Johnson to sign the Civil Rights Act.

Let's get back to cotton for a second: why does it grow so well down here?

It's the fertile soil at the source of "Old Man River," the Mississippi. It's called the Mississippi Delta.

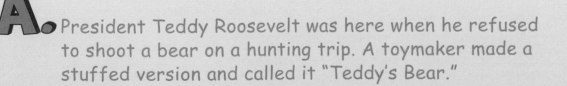

A. President Teddy Roosevelt was here when he refused to shoot a bear on a hunting trip. A toymaker made a stuffed version and called it "Teddy's Bear."

I'll bet you don't even know about all the famous people who come from here—like maybe the most famous woman on TV?

Oprah Winfrey's from Mississippi?

Yup. And some really famous musicians, too; Jimmy Buffett and bluesmen B. B. King, Muddy Waters, and John Lee Hooker. The blues were pretty much invented here in Mississippi. Even the King came from Tupelo.

King of what?

Elvis Presley, you nut! The king of rock and roll!

The blues comes from gospel music, doesn't it?

Right, and it's based in jazz, and some chants and even old field-hand songs. And some of America's best writers are from here. Have you ever heard of a place called Yoknapatawpha County?

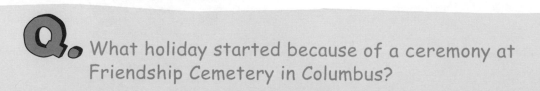

Q. What holiday started because of a ceremony at Friendship Cemetery in Columbus?

Yok—*what*? No, never.

It's a make-believe place author William Faulkner imagined and uses in his books. It's a lot like Oxford, the home of Ole Miss, the University of Mississippi. Richard Wright grew up here, as did Eudora Welty and Tennessee Williams. Southern writers play an important part in our country's literature.

Hey, what's that smell? Actually, I smell a whole bunch of great smells!

It's those people eating dinner under that flowering tree. That's a magnolia, the state flower. And yum, they're all eating delicious local dishes. Shrimp from the Gulf of Mexico, fried catfish, and two kinds of pie.

Sweet potato pie and my favorite, chocolaty Mississippi Mud Pie.

See? We're right back to Old Man River again—it got its name from the muddy banks of the Mississippi River!

Oh, Laura, would you just sit down and have some pie?!

A. On a spring day, the year after the Civil War, townspeople decorated all the soldiers' graves—Confederate and Union—with flowers. This lovely gesture began what we now celebrate as Memorial Day.

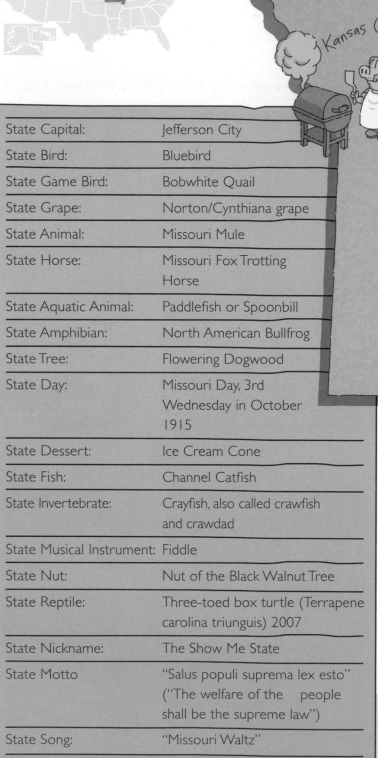

MISSOURI

State Capital:	Jefferson City
State Bird:	Bluebird
State Game Bird:	Bobwhite Quail
State Grape:	Norton/Cynthiana grape
State Animal:	Missouri Mule
State Horse:	Missouri Fox Trotting Horse
State Aquatic Animal:	Paddlefish or Spoonbill
State Amphibian:	North American Bullfrog
State Tree:	Flowering Dogwood
State Day:	Missouri Day, 3rd Wednesday in October 1915
State Dessert:	Ice Cream Cone
State Fish:	Channel Catfish
State Invertebrate:	Crayfish, also called crawfish and crawdad
State Musical Instrument:	Fiddle
State Nut:	Nut of the Black Walnut Tree
State Reptile:	Three-toed box turtle (Terrapene carolina triunguis) 2007
State Nickname:	The Show Me State
State Motto	"Salus populi suprema lex esto" ("The welfare of the people shall be the supreme law")
State Song:	"Missouri Waltz"

Missouri was the 24th state admitted to the United States on August 10, 1821.

 **Q.** Where does the name Missouri come from?

Edward, you know that Missouri is in the Midwest, but there's something about it that only one other state can say.

Ha! You thought I wouldn't know this one, but I do! Like Tennessee, Missouri borders *eight* other states, the most of any state.

Right: "the Show-Me State" is surrounded by Iowa, Illinois, Kentucky, Tennessee, Arkansas, Oklahoma, Kansas, and Nebraska.

Wait, though: why is it called "the Show-Me State"? That's a weird nickname.

Well, there are different stories about the nickname, but mostly people say a congressman once said it in a speech, and he meant he was skeptical and needed to be convinced about things. "I'm from Missouri, and you have got to show me," he said.

That's cool. The people here have some serious 'tude.

I know! You can tell from that arch in St. Louis—have you seen it?

Sure, it's called the Gateway Arch, because we think of St. Louis as the gateway to the West. You know, it's the tallest monument in the whole country, at 630 feet high.

. . . *and* 630 feet wide. C'mon, we can take the tram that's inside and go to the top. What a view—you can see for 30 miles!

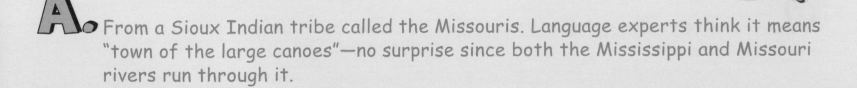

A. From a Sioux Indian tribe called the Missouris. Language experts think it means "town of the large canoes"—no surprise since both the Mississippi and Missouri rivers run through it.

St. Louis is the biggest city in Missouri, but Jefferson City is the capital. How come?

Well, it's right in the middle of the state and on the Missouri River. Those things mattered back in 1821 when they chose it as the capital. It made it easier for people to get to. It was named for Thomas Jefferson, you know.

Right, but he wasn't from here—President Harry S. Truman was. He had a little men's clothing store and didn't even go to college. That's America for you!

Now, you know Mark Twain grew up here in a town called Hannibal. He wrote one of my favorite books ever.

Mine, too! *Adventures of Huckleberry Finn!* Twain's real name was Samuel Clemens, and his hometown was on the Mississippi River, just like Huck's. You know, he was a real riverboat pilot before he became a writer.

Q. You often see new inventions at a world's fair, but this is a delicious one. What was it?

That's right. And three other people came from here that are heroes of mine: Laura Ingalls Wilder, who wrote *Little House on the Prairie,* Walt Disney, and Charles Lindbergh.

That makes sense—the name of the plane "Lucky Lindy" flew across the Atlantic alone was *The Spirit of St. Louis.*

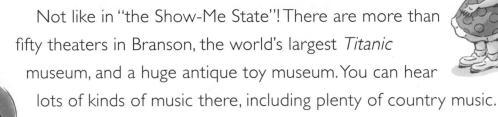

You know, there are a couple of things—kind of odd things—that people come all the way to Missouri to do: shop and see a show.

What do you mean? You can do that anywhere.

Not like in "the Show-Me State"! There are more than fifty theaters in Branson, the world's largest *Titanic* museum, and a huge antique toy museum. You can hear lots of kinds of music there, including plenty of country music.

No wonder the state instrument is the fiddle. What's with the shopping?

All I had hoped to do was to go to Weston and see the Largest Ball of String. It's 19 feet around and over 3,700 pounds.

A. Legend has it that at the St. Louis World's Fair in 1904, the ice-cream cone was invented by rolling up a waffle and putting the ice cream inside!

MONTANA

Montana was the 41st state admitted to the USA on November 8, 1889.

The name comes from the Spanish for "mountainous." Ranching, wheat, lumber, and coal and hard rock mining are primary industries in Montana. Tourism is also important, especially at Glacier National Park and Yellowstone National Park.

Glacier National Park

MONTANA

HELENA

GRIZZLY BEARS!

POMPEY'S PILLAR

LITTLE BIGHORN

Steer Montana

2 TONS!

Jack Horner, a famous paleontologist who works at the Museum of the Rockies in Bozeman, was the real-life inspiration for Dr. Alan Grant in the movie *Jurassic Park.* He was the first scientist to find evidence that dinosaurs cared for their young.

Q. What winter sport made its first American appearance in Lolo Hot Springs in 1965?

State Capital:	Helena
State Bird:	western meadowlark
State Tree:	Ponderosa pine
State Flower:	bitterroot
State Fossil:	duck-billed dinosaur
State Butterfly:	mourning cloak
State Gems:	sapphire and agate
State Fish:	blackspotted cutthroat trout
State Animal:	grizzly bear
State Nickname:	Treasure State
State Motto:	"Oro y Plata" (gold and silver)
State Slogan:	"Big Sky Country"
State Song:	"Montana"

Wow, we're really out West now. Where is everybody?

Well, it's a big state and there are only about six people per square mile. Montana has the lowest population density in the United States. The elk, deer, and antelope outnumber the people!

SIX PEOPLE

ONE SQUARE mile

MONTANA

The capital is named Helena and it was founded just five years before Montana became a state. Like at so many other places, there was a gold rush; a place called Last Chance Creek attracted folks to come here to find their fortune.

Look! The main street is still called Last Chance Gulch. Awesome!

They took gold out of there for about twenty years. By 1888, Helena had fifty millionaires in town, more per capita than any other city in the whole world!

A. The luge, which made its Olympic debut in 1954.

I want to check out Virginia City. It's what was called a boomtown.

What's that?

It's when a town or city springs up really quickly, usually because something valuable is discovered nearby. In the olden days it was often oil, silver or gold.

You mean people see they're going to make good money really quickly, so they just move there?

Exactly, Leo. In the case of Virginia City, prospectors found gold nearby in 1863 and set up a town. Next thing you know, about ten thousand people were living there!

Wow: it sounds exciting!

True, but it was really the Wild West, too. People were greedy, and there were no lawmakers, just vigilantes, who are people who take the law into their own hands.

Well, it sure looks like a ghost town now.

We can stay overnight here, ride a steam locomotive or a stagecoach, and find some neat souvenirs. But there is one more thing.

Q. What animal does Montana more than anywhere else in the forty-eight lower United States?

What?

Um . . . some visitors say it's a *real* ghost town. With, like, *ghosts*. People have reported hearing footsteps on the stage of the old theater, seeing a little girl sitting on the steps of a shop, and an old-timer dressed like a miner, who just vanishes.

OK, I may have had enough of Virginia City. Where to?

How about a trip to Glacier National Park? It's huge, more than a million acres, and this park alone has over three hundred lakes. We can take a ride down this wild road called Going-to-the-Sun Road. It goes across the Continental Divide, and in some places doesn't even have guardrails. It's closed during the winter because of all the snow.

And in the summer it still freaks me out! How did Lewis and Clark do it?

A. The grizzly bear! Every other year a female will have one to four cubs, which weigh only a pound at birth. As cute as they are, don't go near them: she'll attack!

One more stop you'll love before we leave the park: Triple Divide Peak.

What does it divide?

It's called a hydrologic apex. And at this apex, something happens that happens nowhere else in the United States. All the water that runs downhill from here eventually empties into three bodies of water . . .

I know! The Atlantic, Pacific, and Arctic oceans.

Right! Let's go see Pompeys Pillar. On this gigantic piece of sandstone, Native Americans drew petroglyphs, which are images carved on rock. Among them is a carving that says "Wm Clark July 25, 1806."

Is that Clark of the Lewis and Clark Expedition?

Exactly! It's the only proof we still have from their route. He wrote about this in his journal, and here it is!

Why is it called Pompeys Pillar?

You'll remember that Lewis and Clark took along the translator Sacagawea and her tiny baby on the trip. Clark always called the little boy Pompey!

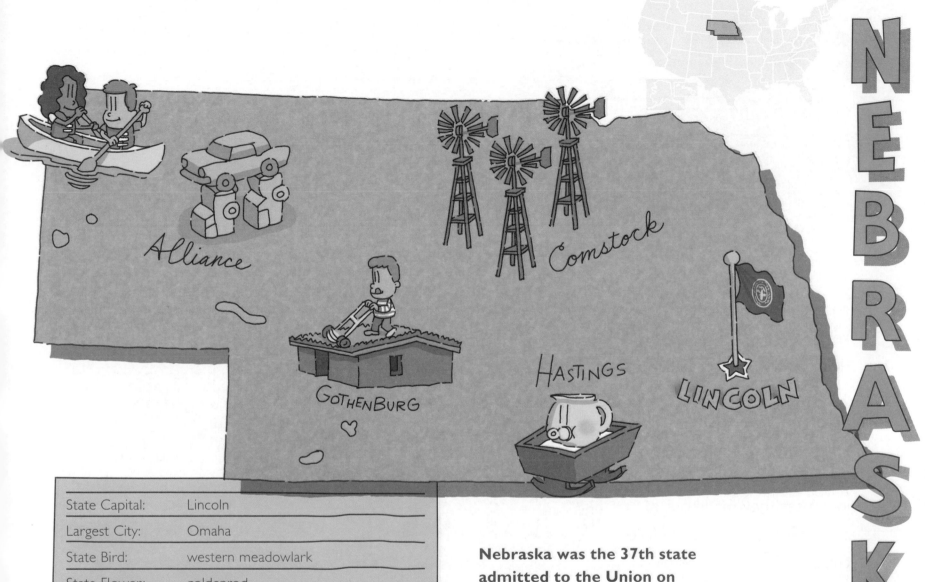

NEBRASKA

Alliance

Comstock

GOTHENBURG

HASTINGS

LINCOLN

State Capital:	Lincoln
Largest City:	Omaha
State Bird:	western meadowlark
State Flower:	goldenrod
State Mammal:	white-tailed deer
State Tree:	cottonwood
State Fish:	channel catfish
State Soft Drink:	Kool-Aid
State Beverage:	Milk
State Nickname:	Cornhusker State
State Motto:	"Equality before the law"
State Song:	"Beautiful Nebraska"

Nebraska was the 37th state admitted to the Union on March 1, 1867.

I guess I know why they call this the Great Plains, Web. It seems like it goes on forever, as far as the eye can see.

I'll bet if you were a homesteader you didn't know whether to be scared or excited.

What's a homesteader?

In 1852, the United States government went back on their word to leave lots of this land to the Indian tribes living here; in the Homestead Act, they made it free to anyone who would come and work on it. If you worked for five years, you could keep 160 acres, which is huge! Nebraska didn't even become a state until 1867, so it was pretty bare out here. People came in droves, many with big families, and were so poor they often lived in houses they made out of sod bricks, and burned buffalo chips for fuel. The wind blew all the time, and they used it for power.

Q. What famous American author wrote about the Great Plains?

These people—they were so brave!

It was free land to farm on. A lot of them were adventurous, and I think a lot of them figured they didn't have any choice. But guess what, Becky? Today Nebraska is all about farming and ranching, so I guess the homesteaders stuck it out!

Why do I feel like I'm seeing Kool-Aid everywhere I look?

You probably are: Edwin Perkins invented it here! He had come up with a bunch of different drinks and figured out a way to take out the liquid, make it a powder, and save on shipping costs. Ta-da—Kool-Aid!

Hey, I know what else is in Nebraska: I saw it in a movie—Boys Town. It was founded in 1921 by a priest named Father Flanagan, for orphaned boys, but now it's turned into a whole town for boys and girls who are in trouble. They come here and go to school, work, play, and get a chance to succeed in life if things are rough at home.

Or if they *have* no home. I loved that movie.

A. Willa Cather was from Red Cloud, and wrote very successful books, such as *O Pioneers!* and *My Ántonia*. Her book *One of Ours* even won the Pulitzer Prize.

One of the most awesome Americans ever also spent time here, starting maybe the greatest traveling show of all time: "Buffalo Bill" Cody. Yee-ha!

Buffalo Bill's Wild West began here? He was unbelievable. He was a Civil War soldier, shot a ton of buffalo to sell the meat to railroad workers—that's how he got his name!—and he received the Medal of Honor as a civilian scout. Then he created the Wild West Show, an ever-changing mix of parades, contests, races, and celebrities of the day, Annie Oakley and Sitting Bull.

He was like a rock star!

No kidding! And one other great American grew up right here in Omaha: Malcolm Little, who became the great human rights activist Malcolm X. Not everyone agreed with his views, but he was one of the most important American black men in history, and was assassinated for his beliefs.

People from Nebraska really live up to their state motto "Equality before the law"!

Q. What Eagle Scout and navel hero from Omaha became the thirty-eighth president of the United States?

A. Gerald R. Ford. Because he became vice president upon the resignation of Spiro Agnew, and president when Richard M. Nixon resigned, he is the only person to hold both offices without ever being elected.

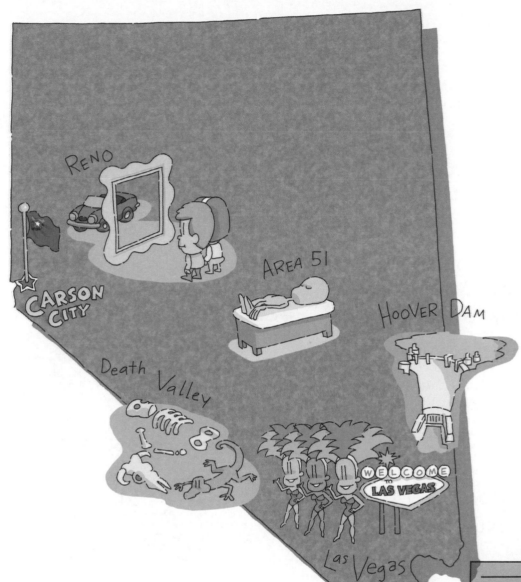

NEVADA

Nevada, America's 36th state, became part of the USA on Halloween in 1864.

The state flag's motto, "Battle Born," refers to the fact that Nevada's admittance to the Union took place during the Civil War.

RENO

AREA 51

HOOVER DAM

CARSON CITY

Death Valley

WELCOME TO LAS VEGAS

Las Vegas

Camels were used as pack animals in Nevada as late as 1870. They could carry more than a horse or mule, and could go without water when traveling across Nevada's Mohave Desert.

State Capital:	Carson City
Largest City:	Las Vegas
State Industries:	tourism, mining (gold and silver), hydro-electric power
State Flower:	sagebrush
State Animal:	desert bighorn sheep
State Bird:	mountain bluebird
State Nickname:	Silver State, Sagebrush State
State Motto:	"All for Our Country "
State Song:	"Home Means Nevada"

F or a state that is mostly desert, you might think Nevada would be boring. Boy, would you ever be wrong!

It's really the Wild West. The capital is Carson City, named after trapper Kit Carson, but it didn't turn out to be the biggest city. About 250 miles away is Las Vegas.

Some folks might say "Vegas" is the wildest city of all. It's famous for gambling casinos and a lot of partying, entertainment, and big shows. "Sin City," they call it, but I think it's fun.

Anita, Vegas isn't even very old. Mobsters came out to the desert in the 1940s because gambling was made legal here and they figured they could make lots of money. And they did!

What's really strange, Chris, is that in this huge, empty desert space, a gigantic man-made marvel has been built.

Q. What is a kangaroo rat?

You mean the Hoover Dam—talk about awesome. Let's go see if they'll let us stand on the top.

I've never seen anything so huge! It was built during the Great Depression, and kept lots of people working. Lake Mead is the reservoir made by the dam; it's the largest man-made reservoir in the United States. When they filled it, they did it slowly, so they wouldn't put too much pressure on the dam. It took six and a half years!

The dam was very dangerous to build—ninety-six men died working on it. They finished more than two years ahead of schedule, even though it was often more than 100°F outside. Just think: there are seventeen generators, and they each can supply electricity to about 100,000 homes. You do the math!

A. An animal that looks like a rat but hops like a kangaroo, it can live in Death Valley its entire life without a drop of water. Temperatures often reach more than 130°F!

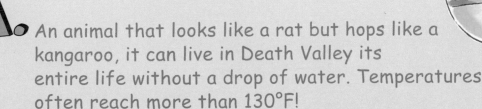

The Hoover Dam and Las Vegas are what everybody knows about Nevada. But there are lots of other incredible things.

My favorite is Area 51.

What's that?

I have one word for you, Chris: aliens! Actually, it's a United State Air Force base, but some funky stuff has happened here. People who believe in extraterrestrials think the government is hiding the fact that spaceships have landed here.

Holy cow! Do you believe in aliens?

Well, I'm not counting them out—just in case!

Here's another place to do with landings, called Elko. It's a little town with an odd piece of history: Elko was the destination of the first commercial airmail flight in 1926. The flight started in Pasco, Washington, and stopped in Boise, Idaho, to pick up some mail on the way.

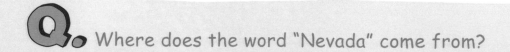

Q. Where does the word "Nevada" come from?

And if that's not odd enough, I'll bet you don't know about the National Cowboy Poetry Gathering.

Cowboy poetry? What!?

I'm not kidding. Think about it: cowboys, cowhands, ranchers—all these people spend lots of time alone in some of the most beautiful places on earth. It makes sense that they'd write down their thoughts about all of it.

Gee, I never thought of it that way. Maybe we should go listen for a while.

Then let's make one more stop— I want to visit Rhyolite; it's an honest-to-gosh ghost town.

No way! Is it haunted?

You'll have to decide that for yourself. But Nevada was a big gold-mining spot, and in 1904 this town sprang up because there was gold nearby. When the gold was gone, the town closed down. In the few years that it was around, there were fifty saloons, fifteen hotels, and ten thousand people.

Now it's just spooky. Man, Nevada sure is full of surprises!

A. It comes from the Spanish for "snowy" or "snow-covered." Although much of the state is desert, Nevada also has mountains that are snow-capped much of the year.

NEW HAMPSHIRE

New Hampshire was the 9th state of the thirteen original colonies admitted to the United States on June 21, 1788. One reason people like to live here is there is no state income tax!

State Capital:	Concord
State Bird:	Purple Finch
State Flower:	Purple Lilac
State Wildflower:	Pink Lady's Slipper
State Tree:	White Birch
State Animal:	White Tail Deer
State Amphibian:	Spotted Newt
State Dog:	Chinook
State Butterfly:	Karner Blue
State Freshwater fish:	Brook Trout
State Saltwater Game Fish:	Striped bass
State Sport:	Skiing
State Fruit:	Pumpkin
State Rock:	Granite
State Nickname:	Granite State
State Motto:	"Live Free or Die"
State Song:	Old New Hampshire

Q. Who was the Old Man in the Mountain?

Boy, this sure is different from Texas, where I'm from.

I guess so! New Hampshire is in New England, and it's mountainous, with rocky soil and really cold winters. Mount Washington in the White Mountains holds the all-time surface wind speed record from back in 1934: a gust of 231 miles an hour blew here during a storm.

What?! Why would anyone want to live here?

New Hampshire is the best! The people here are known for their independent spirit. Even the motto on their license plate is "Live Free or Die."

I like that. What are they so proud about?

They were the first of the thirteen original colonies to declare their independence from England, six whole months before the Declaration of Independence was signed. In fact, everybody agreed the people of New Hampshire should be the first to sign it, because of their bravery.

They were sort of like outlaws!

I know what you mean. Also, this tiny state is very important politically. It's where the first presidential primary election is held. All the candidates come here to campaign months beforehand.

Have any presidents come from here?

Just one: Franklin Pierce. There is even a college named after him here in New Hampshire. He was president just before the Civil War, from 1853 to 1857.

A. It was a series of granite ledges in the White Mountains that looked exactly like a man's face. It collapsed in 2003, but was so popular that a memorial that re-creates it will be built.

I think I need a face lift!

Why do I think there's another great statesman from here?

That would be Daniel Webster. He tried hard to help our country avoid its Civil War, and is thought of as one of the greatest senators and lawyers this country has ever seen. There's even a short story about him I've read called "The Devil and Daniel Webster." He's such a good lawyer that he beats the devil!

The people in this state sound pretty awesome.

No one tells them what to do! Back in 1828, almost four hundred young girls walked out of work at the Dover Cotton Factory because of poor working conditions. It was the first time women had ever gone on strike.

That's brave. Women weren't even given the right to vote until almost a century later.

A lot's changed since then! Let me tell you a little more about New Hampshire. Its capital is Concord, but when people think of this state, they think of its beauty and fun things to do.

Like what? My dog Rufus here and I love a little fun.

Q. Who was Alan Bartlett Shepard Jr. of tiny East Derry, New Hampshire?

Kids from all over the country go to summer camp here. Even though there's only a puny thirteen miles of Atlantic Ocean coastline, camps are all over Lake Winnipesaukee and lots of other lakes.

Oh man! I've never been to summer camp.

You'd love it the rest of the year, too. I learned how to ski when I was only four years old! And you should see how beautiful it is when the leaves change colors in the fall. People come from everywhere just to drive around and see them. They're called "leaf peepers"!

That's funny. It sounds like tourism is important to the state.

It sure is. But remember, it's called "the Granite State," and tons of stone comes from here; lots of headstones you see in cemeteries are made of New Hampshire granite. Also pulp and paper products from all of the forests, and there are farms galore—some are dairy farms, others grow things like corn and fruit. Folks say the first potato in the United States was grown in Londonderry in 1719!

I'm going to see if that cow will give me some chocolate milk!

A. He was the first American ever to travel in space on *Freedom 7*, back in 1961. He was also the fifth person to walk on the moon.

137

NEW JERSEY

New Jersey was the third of the thirteen original colonies to become a state on December 18, 1787. It is named after Jersey, the largest of the Channel Islands, which belonged to England.

State Capital:	Trenton
State Bird:	eastern goldfinch
State Flower:	common meadow violet
State Fruit:	highbush blueberry
State Animal:	horse
State Fish:	brook trout
State Tree:	red oak
State Memorial Tree:	dogwood
State Dinosaur:	Hadrosaurus foulkii
State Insect:	honeybee
State Shell:	knobbed whelk
State Nickname:	Garden State
State Motto:	"Liberty and Prosperity"

Q. What kind of roadside restaurant is especially popular in New Jersey?

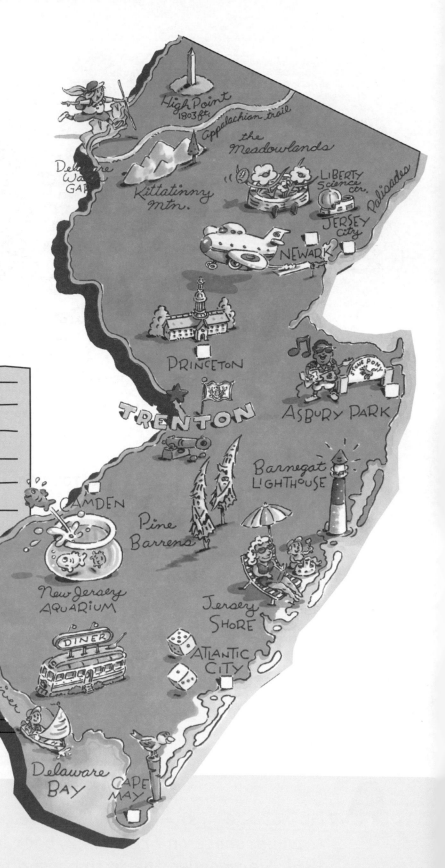

Edward, why do they call New Jersey "the Garden State"? There are lots of cities.

But we also grow a ton of flowers and produce.

Yum. What kinds of food?

Just about everybody agrees the Jersey tomato is about the biggest, juiciest, most delicious you can eat! But we also grow lots of lettuce, corn, blueberries, and cranberries, too, and a weird, fancy salad green called escarole. Plus, the honeybee is our state insect, so there's lots of honey!

I'm confused. I've heard the Meadowlands is a sports stadium, but is it something else, too?

You're right, Sessalee, the stadium's named after the surrounding 8,400 acres of wetlands that has a whole ecosystem of its own. It was a toxic mess for a long time, but now people are making sure it's cleaned up. We can go bird-watching, kayaking, or hiking—sometimes you hear cheers for Jets or the Giants!

A. The diner! There are more than six hundred statewide, considered to be the most of any one place in the world.

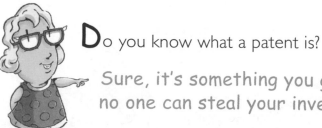

Do you know what a patent is?

Sure, it's something you get from the government so that no one can steal your invention. Why?

Well, a New Jersey man holds the world record: 1,093. Thomas Edison!

No way! I know about the light bulb—but what else?

Well, "the Wizard of Menlo Park" brought us the phonograph, or record player; the ticker tape machine, which printed out stock market prices; and the motion picture camera, to name just a few.

Thomas Edison was in the movie business?!

Yup! He invented the Kinetoscope, a camera that showed objects in motion. Later he built a studio here called the Black Maria, which experts call "America's first movie studio."

Wait: didn't Albert Einstein live in New Jersey, too?

Right—maybe the most famous scientist ever. He studied physics and figured out the theory of relativity. It changed science forever.

Lots of my heroes are from here. Charles

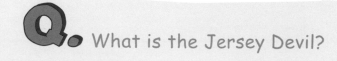

Q. What is the Jersey Devil?

Lindbergh—"Lucky Lindy"—was just a guy who flew an airmail plane, but he became the first man to fly solo, nonstop, across the Atlantic. In his day, he was as famous as a rock star—and that brings me to my other hero: The Boss!

Boss of what?

Bruce Springsteen, Sessalee—that's his nickname!

I know, Edward—I was teasing! Hey, isn't there a town here that has something to do with Monopoly?

That's a funny way to describe it, but sure, you're talking about Atlantic City, or "AC" as some folks call it. It's part of the popular Jersey Shore, and the first boardwalk in the country was built here in 1870. It's got plenty of casinos and hotels, just like Monopoly. And you're right—lots of Monopoly's street names come from here.

I vote we go see the lighthouse my dog Barney is named after on Barnegat Bay, and all go for a swim!

I'll beat you to it!

A. A sort of monster people swear they've seen here for hundreds of years. He supposedly has hooves, a tail, wings, and a head like a horse.

New Mexico became a state on January 6, 1912, the 47th in the Union. Although European explorers and settlers arrived during the 1500s, it is thought that the Clovis culture of Paleo-Indians may have lived here as far back as eleven thousand years ago!

Hot Springs, New Mexico, renamed itself Truth or Consequences when the host of the *Truth or Consequences* TV show said he'd film the popular quiz show from the first town that changed its name.

Q. What is a code talker?

State Capital:	Santa Fe
State Flower:	yucca flower
State Animal:	black bear
State Aircraft:	hot air balloon
State Amphibian:	New Mexico spadefoot toad
State Bird:	chaparral bird or roadrunner
State Butterfly:	Sandia hairstreak
State Cookie:	biscochito
State Gem:	turquoise
State Grass:	blue grama grass
State Insect:	tarantula hawk wasp
State Reptile:	New Mexico whiptail lizard
State Tree:	pine or piñon tree
State Vegetables:	chile and frijol (pinto bean)
State Song:	"O, Fair New Mexico"

There's something about New Mexico I can't put my finger on . . .

I know what it is, Elsa. It looks so unlike many of the other states in America. New Mexico shares a border with Mexico, and so you see lots of that country's influences—the culture, the houses, even the people.

You mean like pueblos, and strings of chiles, and . . .

. . . and like the Whole Enchilada Fiesta in Las Cruces, when fifty thousand people show up to eat the world's biggest enchilada. It's big enough to appear in the Guinness World Records.

Well, no, Scott, I was thinking of something a little more historical, like the Taos Pueblo. *Pueblo* can mean more than house, and in this case it is a village, on a 95,000-acre reservation of the Pueblo people. It's made of adobe—water and straw—and may have been built as long ago as AD 1,000. It is a Taos Indian community. About 150 tribal members live there now, selling pottery and jewelry to visitors.

It's beautiful here. I wouldn't move for a thousand years, either.

A. Many Navajos helped the American war effort during World War II as marines who transmitted to one another messages that the enemy could not understand. They used codes built from their native language.

The people who live in the Southwest are from different ancestors than you see in places like New England, too. Here in New Mexico, almost half are Hispanic, and there are also many Native Americans. And part of the Navajo Nation, which is 26,000 square miles of reservation, is here in the state.

Can you guess one former resident of New Mexico that was none of those things?

Ham, the Astrochimp! In 1961 he flew in a Project Mercury space capsule and performed simple tasks that made NASA realize that it was safe for humans to fly in space. Let's hear it for Ham!

Here's Santa Fe, New Mexico's capital. In the 1800s, this was where the famous Santa Fe Trail ended. It started 1,200 miles away in Missouri, and was it ever dangerous. If the Indians didn't get you for trespassing on their land, the rattlesnakes would! Still, it was the most important route for people here to get things they needed from the North before the railroad was built.

Q. What happened in Roswell, New Mexico, in July 1947?

You know what's also near here? Los Alamos. Talk about secrets and codes and stuff! Los Alamos National Laboratory is one of the biggest labs in the whole world, and during World War II, it was home to the Manhattan Project, which was the code name for building the first atomic bomb. Now they study things like national security and outer space.

You know, it's not exactly outer space, but here's something I think you'd like: the Albuquerque International Balloon Fiesta.

Yikes, I've never seen anything like this! The whole sky is filled with hot-air balloons!

It started in 1972 with just thirteen balloons; now there are more than six hundred. It's the largest event of its kind on earth.

You mean, in the *sky*! Let's go—they let you walk around and peek inside the balloon's basket, and even talk to the pilots. Maybe someone will take us up with them.

A. We may never know for sure, but some folks think that UFOs landed, and that alien bodies were found by the government. People still come there today, looking for clues in the skies.

Hey, you know Ham, the Astrochimp, isn't the only famous animal from New Mexico.

Really? Who else?

Smokey the Bear! Originally Smokey was just a pretend bear in the forest fire prevention ads, but one day firefighters actually found a cub stuck in a tree during a fire. He went to live in the National Zoo in Washington, and was so popular he had his own zip code!

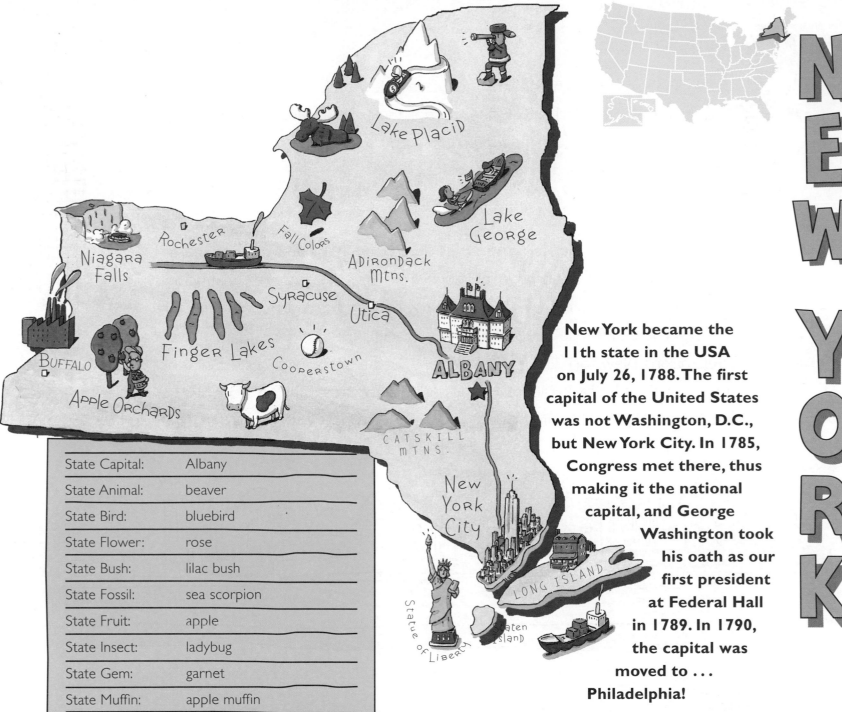

NEW YORK

State Capital:	Albany
State Animal:	beaver
State Bird:	bluebird
State Flower:	rose
State Bush:	lilac bush
State Fossil:	sea scorpion
State Fruit:	apple
State Insect:	ladybug
State Gem:	garnet
State Muffin:	apple muffin
State Reptile:	common snapping turtle
State Shell:	bay scallop
State Tree:	sugar maple
State Nickname:	Empire State
State Motto:	"Excelsior" (Ever upward)
State Song:	"I Love New York"

New York became the 11th state in the USA on July 26, 1788. The first capital of the United States was not Washington, D.C., but New York City. In 1785, Congress met there, thus making it the national capital, and George Washington took his oath as our first president at Federal Hall in 1789. In 1790, the capital was moved to ... Philadelphia!

The first 3-D film, screened before a paying audience, took place at Manhattan's Astor Theater on June 10, 1915.

Julie, I never understood why New York is called "the Empire State."

It was George Washington who first called New York "the seat of the American Empire." New York City's large harbor, the mighty Hudson River, and New York's lush forests and fertile fields all convinced Washington that New York would become an important and wealthy place.

And then the Erie Canal was built, right?

On the button, Kevin. The Hudson River goes north from Manhattan to Canada, but we needed a way to get crops and other products from east to west. The canal wasn't formed by nature, but was built by people. It was the most important public project in New York's history. The 363-mile-long, 40-foot-wide canal linked the Great Lakes to the Hudson River, making New York City the entry port for the entire Midwest. After it opened in 1825, new towns and cities such as Utica, Syracuse, Rochester, and Buffalo sprang up along the canal. Today, the canal is used mostly for sailing and boating.

Q. Who is the most famous Frenchwoman in New York City?

New York is just a beautiful state to be outdoors in.

I like the fall best, when the leaves change color. As the days grow short and there's less sunlight, pigments of leaves start to fade, allowing other bright colors to shine through. Maple trees become giant balls of red and scarlet. Yellow and orange leaves cover elms, butternuts, beech, and ash trees. Red oaks shimmer in deep purple: it's so pretty.

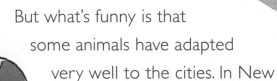

New York's also a great place to see awesome wildlife.

But what's funny is that some animals have adapted very well to the cities. In New York City, pigeons manage to dodge the perils of city life—they're among the toughest birds in the world.

Why don't they fly off to the suburbs?

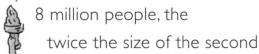

Maybe they love the hustle and bustle of the Big Apple. It's home to more than 8 million people, the largest city in the country. It is more than twice the size of the second largest, Los Angeles.

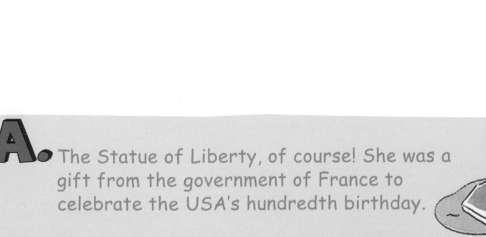

A. The Statue of Liberty, of course! She was a gift from the government of France to celebrate the USA's hundredth birthday.

Let's take a trip up the Hudson River toward Albany and upstate New York.

There sure are a lot of historic towns along the river.

The first Europeans to come to New York settled along the Hudson River. Albany, now the state capital, was the first permanent settlement. It was called Fort Orange. When the Dutch arrived, they built farms and estates along the river. There are some great places to see.

Like where?

We can go to the National Baseball Hall of Fame in Cooperstown. We can see things like Willie Mays's glove, Babe Ruth's bat, and plaques honoring every player in the Hall of Fame.

That sounds like a homerun. Anywhere else?

Tarrytown is home to one of American's first authors, Washington Irving. The nearby town of Sleepy Hollow is where his headless horseman haunted Ichabod Crane.

Q. What famous New Yorker is on all dimes?

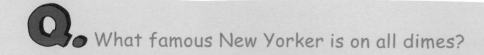

150

What about those other cool towns you mentioned . . . a couple of places that sounded watery?

Oh, right! Saratoga Springs and Lake Placid: two great stops. Saratoga Springs was a vacation spot for the wealthy in the 1800s. People still come in the summer to go to the country's oldest horse racetrack. And Lake Placid has great skiing. It's been home to the Winter Olympics twice!

And here's Niagara Falls—it's incredible!

Forty million gallons of water plunge down every minute. People have been visiting here for nearly two hundred years. Neighbors used to build stockade fences and then charge money to look through holes to see the falls! Today, the power generated from here is used to create 17 percent of New York's electricity.

I wouldn't want to go over those falls.

Lots of people have. The first known person to go over was Anna Edison Taylor in 1901, a sixty-three-year-old schoolteacher who strapped herself to an oak barrel, floated down the river, and fell 180 feet. She made it over and was fine!

Julie, it sounds like New Yorkers have always been explorers of one kind or another!

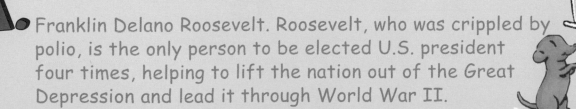

A. Franklin Delano Roosevelt. Roosevelt, who was crippled by polio, is the only person to be elected U.S. president four times, helping to lift the nation out of the Great Depression and lead it through World War II.

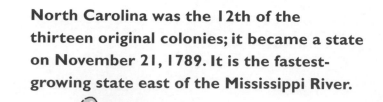

NORTH CAROLINA

North Carolina was the 12th of the thirteen original colonies; it became a state on November 21, 1789. It is the fastest-growing state east of the Mississippi River.

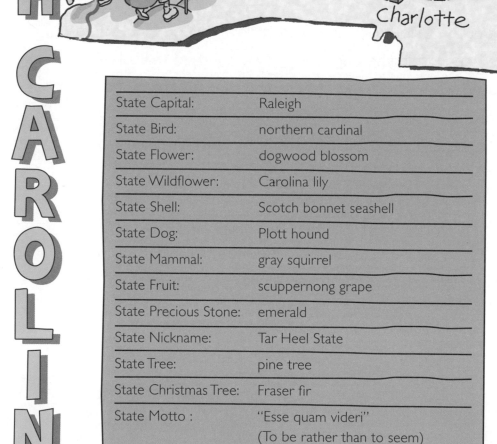

APPALACHIAN TRAIL

RALEIGH

Charlotte

Wright Brothers at KITTY HAWK

Lexington Barbecue FESTIVAL

State Capital:	Raleigh
State Bird:	northern cardinal
State Flower:	dogwood blossom
State Wildflower:	Carolina lily
State Shell:	Scotch bonnet seashell
State Dog:	Plott hound
State Mammal:	gray squirrel
State Fruit:	scuppernong grape
State Precious Stone:	emerald
State Nickname:	Tar Heel State
State Tree:	pine tree
State Christmas Tree:	Fraser fir
State Motto :	"Esse quam videri" (To be rather than to seem)
State Song:	"The Old North State"

Krispy Kreme doughnuts was founded in Winston-Salem in 1937. In the early days, kids would sell them door-to-door, fresh and hot!

Q. What was the Thistle Dhu?

The first thing I think about when I think about North Carolina is two brothers. Do you know who I mean?

I'll bet I can guess: the Wright Brothers.

Yup! Wilbur and Orville. Oddly enough, they got a lot of their ideas about airplane building in a shop they owned in Ohio, working with printing presses and bicycles.

When did they come to Kitty Hawk in the Outer Banks?

In 1903, they finally flew a powered airplane right there on the beach. When Wilbur stayed airborne for 59 seconds and flew 852 feet, that changed the world forever.

A.

The very first miniature golf course was a play on the words "This'll Do." It opened in 1916 in Pinehurst, North Carolina.

153

Speaking of the Outer Banks, we could stay for a while. It has some of the most beautiful beaches in the country; they even let you camp there! Grab your suit and let's go.

Virgina Dare was born near the Outer Banks in the Roanoke Colony in 1587, the first English person in America. Soon afterward, the colony just disappeared. There's evidence it existed, but everyone seems to have vanished.

In 1587? That's way before the Pilgrims. What do you mean, disappeared?

Just what I meant. That's why they call it the Lost Colony.

That's not the only thing that has been lost off the coast of North Carolina. There have been shipwrecks out there: lots of them. So many they call it "the Graveyards of the Atlantic" out there.

Q. Which two presidents were Tar Heels?

154

Scary! Let's go to the Graveyards of the Atlantic Museum on Hatteras Island and find out more, Tex.

We can see cool things recovered from the shipwrecks—even a Nazi Enigma code machine!

Ha! And I thought this was going to be a quiet trip to the beach.

Why do the people from North Carolina call themselves "Tar Heels"?

Good question. Lots of turpentine and tar is made from all the pine trees. During a Civil War battle, soldiers from neighboring states retreated, leaving the North Carolinian troops on their own. When they met the next time, the local troops told the soldiers they'd put tar on their heels to make them stick. When General Robert E. Lee heard this, he said, "God bless the Tar Heel boys."

That's a great story! Today, these Tar Heels lead the nation in plenty of other things. Furniture building, for example: check out the giant chair in Thomasville, and the world's largest chest of drawers in High Point. These Southerners like to do stuff up big!

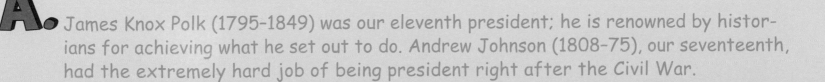

A. James Knox Polk (1795-1849) was our eleventh president; he is renowned by historians for achieving what he set out to do. Andrew Johnson (1808-75), our seventeenth, had the extremely hard job of being president right after the Civil War.

I know North Carolina grows the most tobacco, makes the most bricks, and grows the most sweet potatoes.

Man, they sure are ugly, but I do love sweet potato pie.

There are so many cool cities here. Raleigh is the state capital, Chapel Hill is home to the University of North Carolina, and when you add the city of Durham, it's called "the Research Triangle."

What are they researching, Tex?

These are high-tech businesses: think of it as an East Coast version of California's Silicon Valley.

Hey, I'd like to go to Asheville to see the largest private house in America; it's way bigger than even the White House. It's called the Biltmore House.

Wow! The more than 250 rooms were built by the Vanderbilts in the 1890s; they were one of America's richest families. There's a gigantic indoor swimming pool, funny old-fashioned exercise equipment, a two-story library . . . all kinds of cool stuff. I could totally live here!

State Capital:	Bismarck
State Bird:	western meadowlark
State Flower:	wild prairie rose
State Tree:	American elm
State Fruit:	chokeberry
State Grass:	western wheatgrass
State Motto:	"Liberty and union, now and forever, one and inseparable"
State Nickname:	Peace Garden State, Flickertail State, Roughrider State
State Song:	"North Dakota Hymn"
State March:	"Flickertail March"

North Dakota was the 39th state admitted to the USA; originally part of the Dakota Territory, it became a state on November 2, 1889.

W E

RUGBY

GARRISON DAM

Theodore Roosevelt NATIONAL PARK

BISMARCK

DAKOTA ZOO

JAMESTOWN

*O*ne of my all-time heroines lived in North Dakota until she was chosen to go west with America's most famous explorers. Can you guess who she is, Peter?

Um, no.

Sacagawea! She was a young woman from the Shoshone tribe who went along with the Lewis and Clark Expedition as an interpreter. She carried her tiny baby on her back and proved invaluable. Even though her job was to translate, Lewis and Clark's diaries tell how wise she was during the trip to the Pacific, often providing directions and guidance.

She sounds cool. Is she the woman whose image is on that one-dollar coin?

That's her! Who knows if Lewis and Clark could have made it at all without her? Look, right here is Bismarck; there's a statue of her at the North Dakota Heritage Center.

Bismarck's sort of a funny name for a state capital way out here in the Midwest, don't you think?

There's a reason behind it. It was named after Otto von Bismarck, the chancellor of Germany. The Northern Pacific Railroad decided it was a good name to get people to take the train and move out west.

Q. Who is Louis L'Amour?

That's weird, because now almost one-third of North Dakotans are Norwegian Americans!

That's crazy. There's a town in North Dakota named Rugby.

A town or a sport?

A town. Once again, the railroad named it, this time to attract English settlers. It bills itself as the geographic center of the North American continent.

Cool. You know what else I like? The International Peace Garden. It's half in North Dakota and half in Canada! They plant about a billion flowers here every year, and there's a Peace Tower, half of it in each country. The whole garden is dedicated to world peace—there are even bits of the World Trade Center buried here to remind us.

A. He was an author (1908–88) who wrote 105 books about living in the Old West. He left home as a teenager to experience America, and spent the rest of his life writing about it.

Wow, you can stand in both countries at one time! But I'm pretty sure I have the wildest sightseeing spot in the state: the Enchanted Highway.

Enchanted? How?

An ex-school principal decided to try making metal sculptures—*giant* metal sculptures—to bring tourists to his town of Regent. People loved it! Now you can see seven of them down this 32-mile stretch of road: geese, grasshoppers, a farm family—it's wild.

You know who loved North Dakota? The original Rough Rider, President Theodore Roosevelt. He even worked on a ranch that still exists in Theodore Roosevelt National Park. It's in the middle of the Badlands.

Badlands? What's that?

Dry, dry land, where everywhere you look, things have been eroded by time and rough weather. A lot of times you'll even find fossils there.

Let's go to a big party before we leave— Norsk Hostfest! It's the largest Scandinavian celebration in the world, with clogs, snowflake sweaters, great music and . . .

. . . and Swedish meatballs and something called Viking-on-a-stick. Let's go!

Q. Why is North Dakota a good place to live if you're a bison?

A. Bison, grouse, antelopes, eagles, you name it—they're all protected here in the more than seventy wildlife refuges in the state.

OHIO

Ohio was part of the Northwest Territory and became the 17th state in the Union on March 1, 1803. Interestingly enough, slavery was not permitted in the Northwest Territory for more than sixty years before Abraham Lincoln signed the Emancipation Proclamation.

State Capital:	Columbus
State Bird:	cardinal
State Animal:	white-tailed deer
State Flower:	scarlet carnation
State Wildflower:	large white trillium
State Fruit:	tomato
State Tree:	Ohio buckeye
State Fruit:	pawpaw
State Gem:	Ohio flint
State Reptile:	black racer snake
State Nickname:	Buckeye State
State Song:	"Beautiful Ohio"
State Rock Song:	"Hang On, Sloopy"

Seven United States presidents were born in Ohio: Ulysses S. Grant, Rutherford B. Hayes, James A. Garfield, Benjamin Harrison, William McKinley, William H. Taft, and Warren G. Harding.

Rick, is it true that the French were the first Europeans who explored Ohio, not the British, like the Pilgrims in Massachusetts?

Right, Carla, although Native Americans were here for many centuries before that. In 1669, an explorer and fur trader claimed what's now Ohio for King Louis XIV of France. His name was La Salle—officially René-Robert Cavelier, Sieur de La Salle – and he was probably also the first European to travel the whole length of the Mississippi River.

Wait a minute. Ohio was owned by the French?

Yes, for quite a while. Lots of people in Canada are of French descent, and they came south as pioneers, wanting to settle in what is now American territory. After the French and Indian Wars in the mid-1700s, Ohio became the property of England. Then, after the American Revolutionary War, Ohio became part of the United States.

Wow. A lot of people have been through here in the last few hundred years.

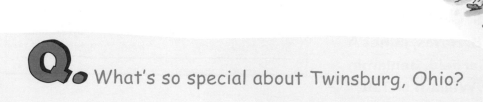

Q. What's so special about Twinsburg, Ohio?

Now say hello to the city of Cleveland, *not* named after an American president, but for General Moses Cleveland, who led the surveying party that founded the city. At one time it was called "the forest city," because it was so densely packed with trees. There's a museum here that is beyond awesome.

Museums are OK. What's so special about this one?

It's the Rock and Roll Hall of Fame and Museum—the only one of its kind in the world! There's tons of stuff to see: instruments, clothes, props, handwritten lyrics, and memorabilia from artists like the Beatles, U2, Elvis, just about everyone!

Rock on!

And there's another worldwide first Cleveland can claim. In 1879, streetlights made an appearance—the first electric ones, not gas lamps. In 1914, they put up the first traffic lights, too!

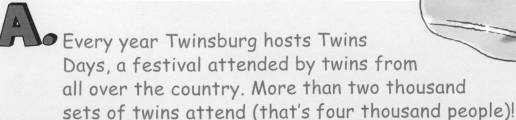

A. Every year Twinsburg hosts Twins Days, a festival attended by twins from all over the country. More than two thousand sets of twins attend (that's four thousand people)!

163

I keep seeing field after field of these short green plants. What are they?

Soybeans, Ohio's biggest crop!

Oh, like soy milk.

Yes, but they're used for a million other things you'd never dream of: candles, tool lubricant, crayons, soap, furniture . . . even socks can be made from soy! The beans are really healthy for you, too; some companies even make hot dogs and ice cream from them.

What's with these people in the horse and carriage?

Have you heard of the Amish? They're a strict religious sect that believes in the simplicity of life. The Amish reject what they call "worldly things," which include a lot of the modern conveniences kids like us are used to.

It sounds like pioneer living!

That's right: many of the Amish don't use cars, or televisions, or even telephones! Amish kids don't go to school beyond eighth grade, because their parents believe that's all the education they need for their simple lives. Ohio has the largest number of Amish, over 200,000 people.

Q. Where is Porkopolis?

I'm getting hungry. Maybe we could stop for a bite to eat.

Great idea. You'll be surprised when I tell you what Cincinnati is famous for: chili!

No way. I thought that was a southwestern dish.

Nope! A man named DeWitt Clinton Pendery invented his own personal chili powder mix, made out of chiles and spices like cumin and oregano. He called it chiltomaline. Then he took it to Texas.

But it really took a twist of its own here in the 1920s, thanks to the Kiradjieff brothers, who figured out all kids of ways to serve chili. Check out the chart and see how many ways you want your chili!

This is a great way to top off a trip to Ohio!

CINCINNATI Chili

3 way SPAGHETTI, CHILI, CHEESE

4 way SPAGHETTI, CHILI, CHEESE, ONIONS OR BEANS

5 way SPAGHETTI, CHILI, CHEESE, ONIONS & BEANS

A. Back in 1835, it's what people called Cincinnati! It was the biggest hog-packing city in the country and you'd see herds of pigs in the streets!

OKLAHOMA

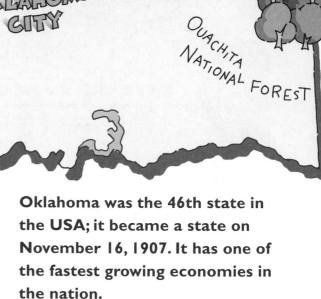

BEAVER

ESKIMO JOE'S

TIRE FACTORIES

TULSA

OKLAHOMA CITY

OUACHITA NATIONAL FOREST

State Capital:	Oklahoma City
State Bird:	Scissor-tailed Flycatcher
State Flower:	Oklahoma Rose
State Wild Flower:	Indian Blanket
State Game Bird:	Wild Turkey
State Tree:	Redbud
State Fruit:	Strawberry
State Vegetable:	Watermelon
State Animal:	Bison
State Game Animal:	White-tail deer
State Flying mammal:	Mexican free-tailed bat
State Furbearer Animal:	Raccoon
State Reptile:	Mountain Boomer
State Cartoon Character:	GUSTY®
State Meal:	Fried okra, squash, cornbread, barbecue pork, biscuits, sausage and gravy, grits, corn, strawberries, chicken fried steak, pecan pie, and black-eyed peas.
State Pin:	"OK" pin
State Poem:	"Howdy Folks"
State Nickname:	Sooner State
State Motto:	"Labor Omnia Vincit" ("Labor Conquers All Things")
State Song:	"Oklahoma!"

Oklahoma was the 46th state in the USA; it became a state on November 16, 1907. It has one of the fastest growing economies in the nation.

Q. What is a panhandle?

Ride 'em, Edward!

What the heck, Sessalee!?

Git along little doggies!

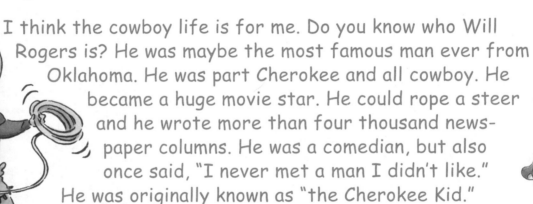

What's this place? The Cowboy Hall of Fame! Whoa, look at that rhinestone guitar! And those awesome chaps!

There are cow*girls* in the Hall of Fame, too, you know. We can learn all about them and the American West right here. There's a Rodeo Weekend, and my personal favorite, the Chuck Wagon Gathering and Children's Cowboy Festival—we can even go on a stagecoach or covered wagon ride.

I think the cowboy life is for me. Do you know who Will Rogers is? He was maybe the most famous man ever from Oklahoma. He was part Cherokee and all cowboy. He became a huge movie star. He could rope a steer and he wrote more than four thousand newspaper columns. He was a comedian, but also once said, "I never met a man I didn't like." He was originally known as "the Cherokee Kid."

Ao It's an elongated piece of land, surrounded on three sides by another entity or place. Oklahoma has a panhandle, as does Florida, Alaska, Connecticut, Idaho, Maryland, Nebraska, Texas—and there are two in Virginia!

Many Cherokees still live here in Oklahoma. After the Civil War, the government took Indian land for white settlers. On April 22, 1889, they offered 12 million acres to anyone who agreed to live on it and improve it. Well, fifty thousand people showed up and the Land Run, as it was called, was set to start at noon. Loads of people snuck in and staked their claim early, which was not allowed. They were called "Sooners," because they took their land too soon.

Sooners? That's what the University of Oklahoma teams are called.

Now you know why.

You know, we've been talking about the cowboys, but Anadarko, Oklahoma, calls itself "the Indian Capital of the Nation." The annual American Indian Exposition is one of the largest gatherings of all the tribes in the country. There will be arts and crafts and tribal dancing—some years there are more than sixty different tribes represented.

Hey, look at all this other stuff around Anadarko: the Southern Plains Indian Museum, Indian City USA, and the American Indian Hall of Fame.

Q. Who are Richard Rodgers and Oscar Hammerstein II?

Indian City shows you how and where Indians lived, and the Hall of Fame has these cool statues, like Tecumseh, Cochise, Sitting Bull, and Jim Thorpe. He was awesome—not only did Thorpe win Olympic medals way back in 1912, he played both professional basketball *and* baseball. Thorpe grew up here in the Sac and Fox nation.

California and Oklahoma have more Native Americans living in them than any other states.

I forget . . . is the capital Oklahoma City?

Yup, it's Oklahoma's largest city, too. And it's a huge economic center for the state. You probably won't be surprised to know that one of the biggest livestock markets in the world is here. But the oil business is in town, too, which means natural gas, petroleum, and oil products.

Oh, sure. What are there, derricks in the center of town?

As a matter of fact, yes! See the state capitol building over there? Take a look at what they call Capitol Site #1.

Wow! There's an oil well right in the yard! Cowboys, Indians, cattle, oil wells—it's really the Wild West in Oklahoma, isn't it, Sessalee?

Yippee-ki-yo, Edward!

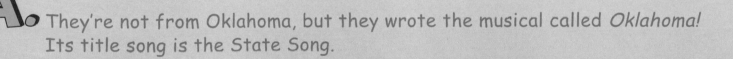

A. They're not from Oklahoma, but they wrote the musical called *Oklahoma!* Its title song is the State Song.

OREGON

Oregon's state flag has an emblem, like so many flags, on the front. However, it is the only state to picture something different on the reverse: the beaver.

HAY STACK ROCK

SALEM

MOUNT HOOD

Pendleton Round-Up

Crater Lake

Malheur National Wildlife Refuge

State Capital:	Salem
State Bird:	western meadowlark
State Animal:	beaver
State Flower:	Oregon grape
State Fruit:	pear
State Tree:	Douglas fir
State Insect:	Oregon swallowtail
State Mushroom:	Pacific golden chanterelle
State Fish:	Chinook salmon
State Nut:	hazelnut
State Nickname:	Beaver State
State Motto:	"She Flies with Her Own Wings" and "The Union"
State Song:	"Oregon, My Oregon"

Oregon was the 33rd state admitted to the USA on February 14, 1859. In the early 1800s, European explorers arrived, seeing a rich future for themselves in trapping and fur trading. John Jacob Astor built Fort Astoria, the first American settlement in Oregon, in 1811 to start his own Pacific Fur Company. It helped make him the first multimillionaire in the country.

Q. Bart didn't grow up here, but his creator did. Who is he?

Here we are in Oregon City, the last stop on the Oregon Trail. It came all the way from Independence, Missouri.

The people who traveled the trail weren't like explorers looking for a waterway or ocean. They were Americans, heading west to a new frontier, moving to new lives.

It wasn't really used for long: from about 1841 to 1869. Then the railroad arrived and everybody took that to get here.

And no wonder, Beau! The trail was almost 2,000 miles long and no one used it in the winter; the terrain was too rough, and there would be less food to find. So everybody who wanted to come west started in the spring, taking four to six months to get here.

Why did it take so long?

The covered wagons full of supplies were pulled by oxen or mules. Oxen typically covered two miles per hour—mules were a little faster. Most people did not ride in the wagon but walked along side. They often collected buffalo dung, which was burned when wood could not be found.

Was the Oregon Trail created by Lewis and Clark on their journey to the Pacific Ocean?

No, the route they went was too dangerous for wagons. However, they spent nearly 8 months in Oregon beginning in 1805 and their maps proved to be invaluable for future settlers.

A. Matt Groening, who grew up in Portland, started writing and drawing *The Simpsons* in 1985. The characters are named after his own family, except for Bart, which is an anagram for "brat."

Did you know that in 1905 in Portland, there was a Lewis and Clark Centennial Exposition to celebrate their expedition from one hundred years before? It was like a World's Fair. They built the biggest log cabin in the world, and it was filled with forestry exhibits.

Speaking of forestry, lumber is big business here in Oregon, isn't it?

Sure is. As far back as the 1780s, a Captain John Meares realized how great the trees were here for masts and spars in ships. He and his men even built a boat here. By 1827, the first sawmill in the Pacific Northwest was built and the lumber industry out here had begun.

Cool. The Homestead Act of 1862 must have helped. The government gave 160 acres to settlers for free, as long as they would work the land. The state needed houses, barns, corrals: all made of wood!

True enough. By 1870, just over forty years after the first one was built, there were 173 sawmills in Oregon.

And not a Home Depot in sight!

Q. What company, in Oregon, tells everyone to "Just Do It!"

But what about the trees that have been cut down? Won't the forests disappear?

Nope. Oregon was the first state in the country to enact a law to make sure there will always be timber. Just a few years ago, 91 million seedlings were planted here.

I'll bet lots of Christmas trees come from here.

Not just a lot: the most! Oregon grows the most of any state!

And lots of salmon. And get this: the beaver, which is the state animal, actually helps the salmon in all kinds of ways by building dams. For example, the dams make pools where young salmon can live and avoid dangerous predators.

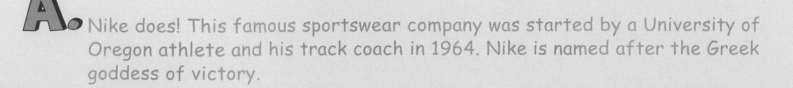

A. Nike does! This famous sportswear company was started by a University of Oregon athlete and his track coach in 1964. Nike is named after the Greek goddess of victory.

Remind me, Penny: isn't there something weird about the salmon?

Y ou're probably thinking about their swimming upstream, but that's just a part of it. They're spawned, or born, in streams, and when they're young, they swim out to the ocean. Weird already, because they can live in both salt and fresh water: most fish can't do that. Then they grow up and live out in the ocean, sometimes for years. When it's time to spawn their own babies, they swim upstream to the *exact* spot where *they* were born! And before you ask, no, we don't know how they know to do that!

HMMM... THIS PLACE LOOKS FAMILIAR.

Home Sweet Home

But we *do* know Oregon has one of the largest salmon-fishing industries in the world. And for something that's the smallest, try Mill Ends Park!

Where's that?

In Portland. It's 2 feet around, and was built in 1948 on Saint Patrick's Day: for leprechauns and snail races!

Beau, you're as nutty as whoever designed that crazy park!

Pennsylvania became the second state in the Union on December 12, 1787. Pennsylvania originated when King Charles II granted a land charter to William Penn as a result of a debt he owed to Penn's father. The state's name means "Penn's woods," in honor of Admiral Penn.

Pennsylvania was the first state to list their Web site's URL on their license plates.

State Capital:	Harrisburg
State Game Bird:	ruffed grouse
State Flower:	mountain laurel
State Tree:	eastern hemlock
State Plant:	penngift crownvetch
State Animal:	white-tailed deer
State Beverage:	milk
State Dog:	Great Dane
State Fish:	brook trout
State Insect:	firefly

State Electric Locomotive:	GG1 4859 Electric Locomotive
State Steam Locomotive:	K4s Steam Locomotive 1987
State Cookie:	chocolate chip
State Toy:	Slinky
State Nickname:	Keystone State
State Motto:	"Virtue, Liberty, and Independence"
State Song:	"Pennsylvania"

PENNSYLVANIA

I don't know much about Pennsylvania, Josh.

Let's start with Pittsburgh. Before there were any cities, lots of action took place on or near the rivers. Pittsburgh's Ohio River played a big part in the French and Indian War.

What did the French have to do with Americans?

The Indians had been living here for centuries, when the French came down the Ohio River in 1669. Before long the British showed up, and suddenly they both wanted control of this beautiful land. The British built Fort Pitt here, and with the Indians on their side, defeated the French. With the American Revolution, the land became ours.

And now it's "the Steel City!"

Or "the City of Bridges." Guess how many there are.

Um . . . seventeen?

Q. What does the Just Born Company in Bethlehem produce?

Nope, there are 446! Only Venice, Italy, has more. Until some bad economic times in the 1970s, steel was one of the biggest businesses in U.S. history. Pittsburgh steel built the Empire State Building and the Golden Gate Bridge!

Coal mining has also been huge in Pennsylvania.

What is coal, anyway?

It's what's called a fossil fuel. It's formed over long periods of time from plants that were near water and became rock. Miners dig it out of the earth. Now we know that burning coal isn't very healthy for people or the environment.

Sounds like you'd have to be pretty brave to be a miner, going underground like that.

You bet, Becky. Let's go over to the Pioneer Tunnel Coal Mine in Ashland—we can ride the steam train and see.

A. It the home of Peeps. People eat enough Peeps candy chicks every year to circle the earth if you put them beak to tail!

Is this the real Gettysburg battle-field?

Yes. For three days in 1863, the Northern states fought the Southern states during the Civil War in the bloodiest battle ever on American soil. About fifty thousand soldiers were killed.

That's when Lincoln gave the Gettysburg Address.

Right. As far as speeches go, it was pretty short—only ten sentences! He wanted everyone to know that the United States would survive and that everyone would be free. That's why he said that the government "of the people, by the people, for the people, shall not perish from the earth." President Lincoln was saying that whether you were from the Union or the Confederacy, black or white, everyone was considered equal, like the Declaration of Independence says.

I'd like to see the real Declaration of Independence. Is it in Philadelphia?

Sure is! Let's visit Independence Hall—the Constitution is there, too.

What's the difference between them?

The Declaration of Independence was written by Thomas Jefferson in 1776. It pretty much told King George III of England that we intended to be

Q. Why was the United States' first world's fair in Philadelphia?

free. The Constitution, written in 1787, is like a map of our laws. It's a really smart outline of how the country should run.

We haven't even talked about Philadelphia's most famous resident, Benjamin Franklin!

He's what we call one of the Founding Fathers. He's famous for his work helping to form our nation, but also because he was about the smartest person and inventor you can imagine.

He figured out the whole electricity thing, with the kite and key.

That's not all. He invented bifocal glasses, swim fins, the Franklin stove, the lending library, the first volunteer fire department and fire insurance company, and the odometer, which measures distance!

Wait! And then there's Betsy Ross!

She owned an upholstery business and George Washington asked her to make a flag for our new country. This is when it was decided to have thirteen stripes for the original colonies and a star for every state.

I guess this is also my last chance to have a famous Philly Cheesesteak sandwich.

Yummm . . . grilled steak, fried onions, and Cheez Whiz. I never want to leave Pennsylvania!

 A. It was to celebrate our country's first hundred years, or centennial, in 1876. The telephone, typewriter, and Heinz ketchup were first presented here to a fascinated audience.

RHODE ISLAND

State Bird:	Rhode Island Red
State Flower:	violet
State Tree:	red maple
State Fruit:	Rhode Island greening apple
State Drink:	coffee milk
State Fish:	striped bass
State Mineral:	bowenite
State Rock:	Cumberlandite
State Shell:	quahog
State Yacht:	Twelve-meter yacht *Courageous*
State American Folk Art:	Charles I. D. Looff Carousel
State Nickname:	Ocean State, Little Rhody
State Motto:	"Hope"
State March:	"Rhode Island"
State Song:	"Rhode Island It's for Me"

The state's original name was "Rhode Island and Providence Plantations" because it was a merger of two colonies. Despite being to first state to renounce its allegiance to the British Crown, it was the last of the 13 original colonies to become a state, on May 29, 1790.

Q. What was special about Slater's Mill in Pawtucket?

Well, Rhode Island can claim something that no other state in the Union can. Know what it is, Web?

Of course—it's the smallest state! Little but awesome. Like me.

Oh, brother. Well, then, you'll like this: Rhode Island was founded by a rebel named Roger Williams. He came from England and was a pastor in Massachusetts, but he didn't last there long. He had different religious views than his superiors, and believed that all people should be allowed to practice the kind of religion they want. Almost 150 years later, Thomas Jefferson and John Adams said Williams's ideas about separation of church and state as well as freedom of speech helped them write the Bill of Rights.

I know about Roger Williams. He also wanted to get rid of slavery and treat the Native Americans like equals, too. In fact, Rhode Island was the first place in all of North America to outlaw slavery, way back in 1652. That's more than two hundred years before the Civil War.

A. In 1793, it started America's Industrial Revolution by being the first water-powered cotton mill in the United States.

Because of Roger Williams and all the early settlers in Rhode Island, there are a lot of "firsts" here that beat out all the other states.

Cool! Like what?

Like the oldest schoolhouse, the oldest Baptist church, the oldest synagogue, and Pawtuxet, the oldest village.

I know one more: Battle of Rhode Island, in which the very first African-American regiment fought.

We've talked about a lot of history, but Rhode Island is a really fun state, too.

No kidding—it's called "the Ocean State" for a reason. It has a ton of beaches, and Newport is one of the greatest sailing capitals in the whole world. Really wealthy people used to build gigantic summer houses here. They were called "cottages," but they were huge mansions!

People love sports here, I guess. The Tennis Hall of Fame is right here in Newport. The first golf tournament was in Rhode Island, as was the first polo match.

There are other horses you can ride. If you visit a tiny town called Watch Hill, you can still ride on the Flying Horse Carousel, which is the oldest in the country.

Q. What kind of poultry is named after this New England state?

But I hear the best thing of all is Bristol's Fourth of July Parade. It's also the oldest one in the United States; it first started in 1875, and you can't miss the route. They paint huge red, white, and blue stripes right down the middle of the street!

OK, this is a test. Rhode Island isn't really an island, of course . . . but there *is* an island that's part of Rhode Island. What is it?

I know that one: Block Island!

Right! Block Island has a giant old hotel and a big sailing race in the summer.

There are also some delicious seafood treats Rhode Islanders eat. I'll bet you know about quahogs.

Wait, isn't Quahog the name of the town where Stewie and the Griffins live on *Family Guy*?

Well, Seth MacFarlane, who writes *Family Guy,* went to college in Rhode Island, so he made that up. But a stuffed quahog is really a yummy giant clam all chopped up with stuffing—that's why locals call it a "stuffie."

Give me one of those and some clam cakes and I'll visit here any old time!

A. The Rhode Island Red, a chicken so popular it has its own statue in Adamsville, Rhode Island!

State Capital:	Columbia
State Bird:	carolina wren
State Wild Game Bird:	wild turkey
State Flower:	yellow jessamine
State Wildflower:	goldenrod
State Tree:	sabal palmetto
State Fruit:	peach
State Animal:	white-tailed deer
State Dog:	boykin spaniel
State Hospitality Beverage:	tea
State Snack Food:	boiled peanuts
State Lowcountry Handcraft:	sweet grass basket
State Music:	the spiritual
State Opera:	"Porgy and Bess"
State Dance:	The Shag
State Shell:	lettered olive
State Nickname:	Palmetto State
State Motto:	"Dum Spiro Spero" ("While I breathe, I hope")
State Song:	"Carolina," and "South Carolina on My Mind"

South Carolina became the 8th state of the United States on May 23, 1788. It was the first state to secede from the Union prior to the Civil War.

Q. What's so odd about the shape of Hilton Head Island?

Wow! This is some crazy way to enter a new state! What the heck is this place, Lorraine?

I knew you'd like it. It's called South of the Border. My mom told me about it: she came here on a road trip once back in the 1970s! Everyone stops here; you can get cool souvenirs, stay over in a hotel— there's even an amusement park.

Oh boy, we can even buy fireworks! They scare my dog Maggie a little, but not me!

We're in South Carolina, "the Palmetto State," just "south of the border" from North Carolina. It gets its nickname from all the beautiful palm trees here.

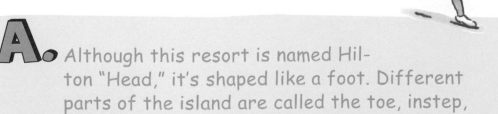

A. Although this resort is named Hilton "Head," it's shaped like a foot. Different parts of the island are called the toe, instep,

Palm trees? I guess it stays pretty warm here.

It's what called a humid subtropical climate, which means it gets really hot and steamy in the summer and hardly ever snows in the winter. The state capital is Columbia, and it was probably chosen as South Carolina's major city way back in 1786 for two reasons. The first is because it's in the middle of the state, so in the old days, it made it a good central meeting place. The second reason has to do with geography.

Ugh. I hate geography.

But this is interesting. Columbia is at what's called a fall line. That's a place where it gets too hard to navigate upstream on a river—that's the bad news—but also creates waterfalls or rapids, something that makes the water so strong that you could put a water mill, or these days, a dam or generator.

OK, I admit that is pretty cool.

And there's an awesome zoo here called Riverbanks. It has more than three thousand animals and birds; and if you like weird plants, there's a botanical garden, too.

What kinds of animals? I've been to zoos before.

Get this: like koala bears, snakes, birds, grizzly bears, warthogs—we can even go to the animal hospital and kitchen.

Q. Who are three famous Jacksons from South Carolina?

Huh? Zebras don't cook!

I think the prettiest city in the state—some say in the whole South—is Charleston. And if it seems like everything's clean and people are really polite, it's true: Charleston started the first "Livability Court," so you have to control your garbage, your pets—even your noise!

Maggie, you'd better behave. I hear some of the carriage tours even have their horses wear diapers so they don't dirty the street in front of the mansions.

The old houses are so beautiful here, but some of Charleston's history is not. South Carolina was the first state to secede from the Union before the Civil War. Cotton was king then, and most of the people living here, or nearby on plantations, were slaves. That war ended slavery and reunited the North and South, but many people died. The very first shots of that war were fired here in Charleston.

A. Andrew, the seventh president of the United States; Jesse, the famous civil rights activist and friend of Dr. Martin Luther King Jr.; and "Shoeless Joe," a famous outfielder from the 1920s who still holds the third-highest major-league batting average.

This must have been a dangerous spot, with the fort being on the water.

Yeah, but there's a sort of funny story about another fort near here, called Fort Moultrie. During the Revolutionary War, the British fired cannonballs at it, but because it was built with soft, spongy logs from the palmetto tree, they bounced right off!

No wonder they call it "the Palmetto State." Maybe the tree saved everyone!

South Carolina's coast is so pretty. A lot of it's called the Grand Strand—this 60 miles of beaches is one of the most popular tourist places in the country.

Maggie and I both love the beach—let's go! What town is this?

Myrtle Beach. There's an amusement park here, lots of golf courses, fishing, about a billion restaurants to try, and lots of beachy fun. Let's go swimming!

A state that has South of the Border and a ginormous beach? I think South Carolina is for me!

State Capital:	Pierre
Largest City:	Sioux Falls
State Bird:	ring-necked pheasant
State Flower:	American pasque flower
State Animal:	coyote
State Fish:	walleye
State Bread:	fry bread
State Tree:	Black Hills spruce
State Nickname:	Mount Rushmore State
State Motto:	"Under God, the people rule"
State Slogan:	"Great Faces. Great Places."
State Song:	"Hail, South Dakota"

South Dakota was admitted to the union on November 2, 1889, as the 40th state. "Dakota" comes from the name the Sioux Indians used for themselves.

I can't wait. At last I'm going to get to see my favorite American monument: Mount Rushmore!

I can't believe we're here in the Black Hills! Look at it, Edward—it's huge. Just the noses alone are 20 feet high; that's almost five times my height.

A man named Gutzon Borglum sculpted them, but what he did seems more like constructing a building than sculpting. It took four hundred men to build Mount Rushmore, from 1927 all the way to 1941. Workers had to climb 506 steps just to start work each morning; by the time it was all done, they had cut away 800 million pounds of stone!

Two million people come to visit here every year. Hey, Edward, close your eyes, and quick tell me which presidents are carved here, from left to right.

That's easy: George Washington, Thomas Jefferson, Teddy Roosevelt, and Abraham Lincoln. They represent the first 150 years of America's history.

Don't forget, there's the Crazy Horse Memorial only a few miles away, too. The Native Americans wanted a monument to the great Lakota chief; it reminds us that they lived on this soil thousands of years before the white man came along.

Q. What is kuchen?

KUCHEN

Who's Pierre?

What? Pierre who?

I don't know; that's why I'm asking *you*. Pierre just seems like a weird name for a state capital.

Oh, *that* Pierre! It's named after a famous fur trader, Pierre Chouteau Jr. He built what was probably the most important fur trading post and fort in the Great Plains. He was just fifteen when he started his own fur-trading business. This location was chosen for the capital because it's both in the middle of the state and on the Missouri River.

That old mining town, Deadwood, is in South Dakota, too. Do you know how it got it name? From all of the dead trees surrounding it.

NOW THAT'S A KILLER HAND!

Deadwood has become famous because there is both a novel and a television show about it. Wild Bill Hickok was killed here, while playing poker in a saloon. When he was shot, he was holding two aces and two eights, which is now known as the "Dead Man's Hand."

Yikes! He was awesome, though: one of the first real heroes of the Old West. He's buried right here in Deadwood.

 It is German for "cake" and many different kinds have been popularized by German immigrants. The version that features a doughy crust and custard filling is the State Dessert of South Dakota.

There's one more thing I have to see: it's in Mitchell, South Dakota.

I know what it is: the first Corn Palace!

That's it! One of three, it was built for the Corn Belt Exposition in 1892.

Every year, a local artist totally redesigns the outside—and it's all made of corn. There are themes, like Lewis and Clark, or Everyday Heroes.

Here's something funny. You know the Corn Palace is used as a sports arena sometimes, and Mitchell High School plays basketball here. Their team's name is . . . the Kernels!

Q. What do woolly mammoths have to do with South Dakota?

A. In 1974, bones of fifty-five fossils who died twenty-six thousand years ago were unearthed here. They can be seen at the Mammoth Site in Hot Springs.

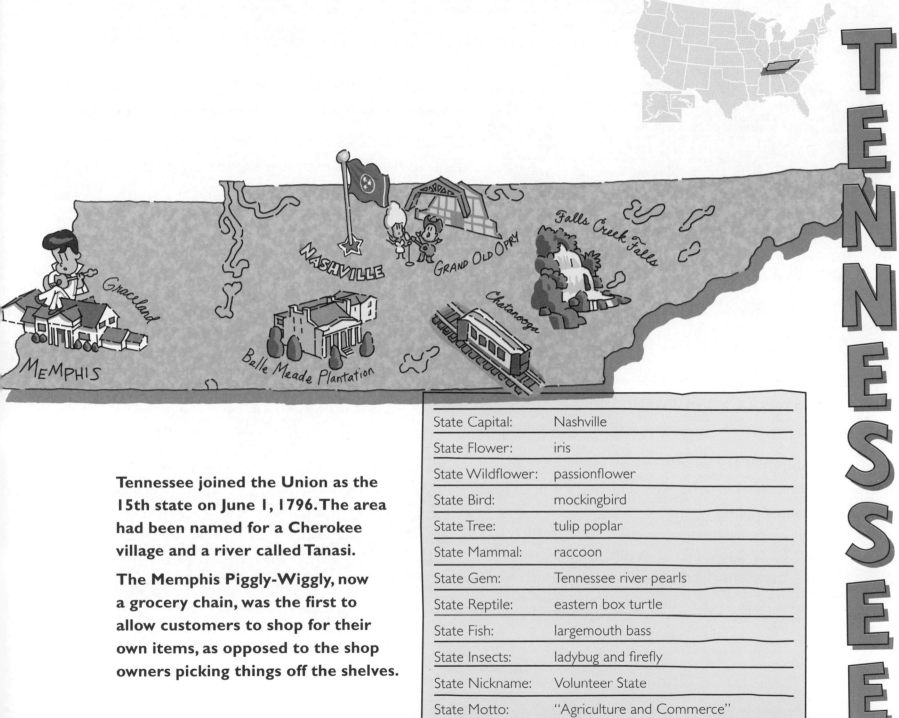

Tennessee joined the Union as the 15th state on June 1, 1796. The area had been named for a Cherokee village and a river called Tanasi.

The Memphis Piggly-Wiggly, now a grocery chain, was the first to allow customers to shop for their own items, as opposed to the shop owners picking things off the shelves.

State Capital:	Nashville
State Flower:	iris
State Wildflower:	passionflower
State Bird:	mockingbird
State Tree:	tulip poplar
State Mammal:	raccoon
State Gem:	Tennessee river pearls
State Reptile:	eastern box turtle
State Fish:	largemouth bass
State Insects:	ladybug and firefly
State Nickname:	Volunteer State
State Motto:	"Agriculture and Commerce"
State Songs:	"My Homeland Tennessee," "The Tennessee Waltz," "When It's Iris Time in Tennessee," "My Tennessee," "Rocky Top, Tennessee," and "The Pride of Tennessee"

193

Here we are in Tennessee! Why do they call it "the Volunteer State?"

During the War of 1812, two thousand men from Tennessee volunteered to fight for General Andrews Jackson's militia—he would later become our seventh president. Some of the men were Choctaw Indians or black, and that was unusual. Years later, when they were asked to sign up to help fight the Mexican-American War, the men here stepped up again.

They have a reputation for bravery. Davy Crockett was from Tennessee, too, and he was plenty brave! They called him King of the Wild Frontier.

"Fellow Congressmen."

He was a congressman, too. Tons of stories are told about him as a hunter and trapper, and to tell the truth, he may have made some up. He's what we call a folk hero: he was real, but some of his tales were pretty tall!

I don't care, Anita. I wish I had one of those awesome coonskin caps.

Q. "Fairy floss" was what this Tennessee invention was originally called. What is it called now?

Davy Crockett was not the only "King" here in Tennessee. The King of rock and roll, Elvis Presley, moved to Memphis as a teenager, and when he became famous, lived in a mansion called Graceland.

We can go there: it's now a museum. Except for the White House, this is the most visited private home in America. It's full of his sequined jumpsuits, gold records, awards, and even some of his famous cars.

Look! There's Elvis's old pink Cadillac!

One of the saddest things in American history happened in Memphis, too, though.

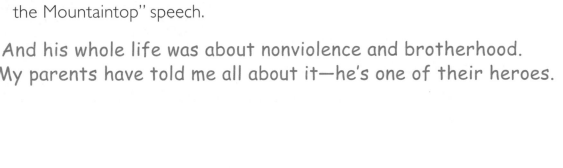

That's right, Chris. The great civil rights leader Reverend Martin Luther King Jr. was shot and killed right here, just a day after he gave his famous "I've Been to the Mountaintop" speech.

And his whole life was about nonviolence and brotherhood. My parents have told me all about it—he's one of their heroes.

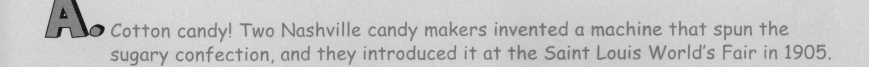

A. Cotton candy! Two Nashville candy makers invented a machine that spun the sugary confection, and they introduced it at the Saint Louis World's Fair in 1905.

Music is huge everywhere in Tennessee. Some say country music started here, but one thing is for sure: it's home to the Grand Ole Opry in Nashville.

I know about that—my grandma listens to their show. She says it's the oldest radio program in the world and that it's been on every Saturday night since 1925. Let's take in a show at the Grand Ole Opry House.

It also would be fun to go to the Great Smoky Mountains.

You bet, and we wouldn't be the only ones; it's the most visited national park in the country. Did you know the "smoke" or fog that you see hanging over them is warm air blown all the way up from the Gulf of Mexico?

That's awfully far. Entire towns were moved out of here to make it a national park. Cades Cove, the most popular place in the park, is still filled with old homesteads and churches. We can stay over in a cabin.

Q. What Tennessee town was state capital for one day in 1792?

Good. That way the black bears won't get us!

We might see bears, but they're important. The Smokies are part of what's called an International Biosphere Reserve, land meant to try to maintain a balanced ecosystem. There are more than ten thousand species of animals and plants that we know about in the park.

Hmmm . . . Well, if I discover a new snake, I want credit! How about we go where *I'd* like to go now: Dollywood!

I can't imagine a better combination than Dolly Parton and an amusement park!

Dolly was determined to follow her dream, so the minute she got out of high school, she headed for the Grand Ole Opry.

And look where it got her! Now we have a one-of-a-kind Smoky Mountain adventure, with a giant wooden roller coaster, great music, and crafts, from blacksmithing to glass blowing to wood carving!

A. Kingston. The Tennessee General Assembly moved it there for a day to comply with a promise they had made to the Cherokees. Having kept their promise, they promptly moved it back to Knoxville.

TEXAS

Texas became the 28th state in the Union on December 29, 1845. Texas once belonged to Mexico, but its citizens desperately wanted their independence. Even after they gained their freedom from Mexico, people were divided as to whether they wished to remain independent, or become part of the United States.

State Capital:	Austin
State Bird:	mockingbird
State Flower:	bluebonnet
State Tree:	pecan
State Plant:	prickly pear cactus
State Dog Breed:	Blue Lacy
State Dish:	chili
State Footwear:	cowboy boot
State Fruit:	Texas red grapefruit
State Large Mammal:	longhorn
State Small Mammal:	nine-banded armadillo
State Musical Instrument:	guitar
State Snack:	tortilla chips and salsa
State Sport:	rodeo
State Vegetable:	sweet onion
State Vehicle:	chuckwagon
State Nickname:	Lone Star State
State Motto:	"Friendship"
State Song:	"Texas, Our Texas"

GREAT PLAINS

Amarillo

Red River

RODEOS

GUADALUPE MTNS NATIONAL PARK

FORT WORTH

Dallas

COMPUTER INDUSTRY

Trinity River

Colorado River

AUSTIN

Rio Grande

CATTLE RANCHES

OIL RIGS

Houston

BIG BEND NAT'L PARK

THE ALAMO

San Antonio

JOHNSON SPACE Center

Corpus Christi

Brownsville

The King Ranch in Texas is bigger than the state of Rhode Island.

Q. What almost started a war between Texas and France in the 1830s?

I'm a little confused. Was Texas in Mexico or were Mexicans in Texas?

Good question, Meredith, and the answer is, a little bit of both! Of course, the Native Americans were here before anyone, about ten thousand years ago. More recently, Texas used to be a part of Mexico; but then a lot of folks from the United States moved down here, and didn't want to stay under Mexican rule. So it's no wonder today you see so many Texas residents who are of Mexican descent.

When I think of Texas, I think, "Remember the Alamo!" But I don't really even know what that means.

The Alamo is a fort where 189 heroes fought for Texan independence. It was built in the 1700s as a religious mission, when Texas was still part of Mexico. By 1836, Texans wanted to be free from Mexican rule. This small band of men guarding the fort, including the legendary Davy Crockett, held off five thousand Mexican soldiers for thirteen days before they were defeated; every single man inside the Alamo was killed. So when the two warring groups met again just a few weeks later, the Texan rebels charged into battle shouting, "Remember the Alamo!" And guess what? This time, the Texans won, and gained their independence.

. Pigs! War was almost declared after roving groups of pigs entered the French embassy and ate beds and important papers.

Tex, is there really such a thing as a roadrunner, like in the cartoons?

Yup! You'll find roadrunners scurrying through the desert, zipping along at 20 miles per hour. Just as in the cartoon, they go, "Beep! Beep!" And we have armadillos, the oddest of all. They are the size of a house cat and can run as fast as you can. But they can't hear or see well, which is sometimes why you see them as roadkill!

When I think of "the Lone Star State," I think of cattle and oil.

During the 1800s, ranchers moved into the High Plains part of Texas, where its wide open spaces and warm weather are perfect for cattle. By 1860, there were six cows to every one person in Texas! It was the cattle trade that helped rebuild Texas after the Civil War. For a long time, cows just ran wild, but the invention of barbed wire brought fences, ending the era of roundups on the range. The cattle drives were gone.

Who discovered there was so much oil in Texas?

In 1901, two drillers named Patillo Higgins and Anthony Lucas punched a hole in an underground salt dome, in a place called Spindletop, in eastern Texas. Oil gushed out, soaring higher than a twenty-story building. That's when the oil boom hit. Thousands of drillers dug deep into the ground looking for "black gold." Huge companies emerged, like Exxon, Texaco, and Chevron.

Q. What part of Houston is out of this world?

Was Houston built with oil money?

It sure was. Today, it's a huge center for the oil industry, with oil refineries, petrochemical manufacturers, and a gigantic harbor. It had been a sleepy little town on a swamp at the edge of Galveston Bay. Being on a swamp, Houston was a hot, muggy place, and not a pleasant place to live in. Then air-conditioning was invented in the 1930s, and the population went from 100,000 to a million in twenty years!

Does Texas produce more oil than the other states?

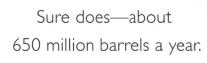

Sure does—about 650 million barrels a year. And imagine: an 1899 geological survey said there was "little or no chance for oil . . . in Texas!"

What else is in Houston besides oil?

Lots of stuff, Meredith. The nation's largest cattle show and second largest rodeo are held here.

A. The Johnson Space Center! The National Aeronautics and Space Administration—or NASA—uses it to direct all manned space missions, train astronauts, and build space equipment.

Tex, tell me a little about the rodeo.

*R*odeo mean "roundup" in Spanish. It dates back to the 1700s, when cowboys used to perform tricks as entertainment. When barbed wire closed the open ranges and the cattle drives—or roundups—stopped, people still wanted to see cowboys perform their tricks. Almost every large town and city holds rodeos today—and that's all over the country, not just where there are cowboys and cattle. Modern-day rodeos include calf-roping, livestock shows, riding contests, bucking broncos, and more.

Do you want to be a cowboy when you grow up, Tex?

No way! People have a pretty romantic picture of a cowboy's life. That image comes from artists, writers, and later, filmmakers who portray them as heroic men on the frontier. It's a hard and lonely job. I'm just happy to be from Austin and to say, "Don't mess with Texas!"

Statehood for Utah was originally proposed in 1849 under the name of Deseret and would have included land currently in Colorado, Idaho, Nevada, Wyoming, Arizona, Oregon, New Mexico and California. It was rejected for being too large with too few settlers. Statehood was granted to Utah on January 4, 1896, the 44th state.

State Animal:	Rocky Mountain elk
State Bird:	California seagull
State Cooking Pot:	Dutch oven
State Emblem:	Beehive
State Flower:	Sego lily
State Fruit:	cherry
State Gem:	topaz
State Mineral:	copper
State Motto:	"Industry"
State Rock:	coal
State Tree:	blue spruce
State Vegetable:	Spanish sweet onion
State Song:	"Utah, This Is the Place"

I love being out west. I've never been to Utah, though.

We're going to have a ball. Funny thing is, it's huge, but almost 80 percent of the people in Utah live in or around Salt Lake City, the capital. Even so, New York City has almost three times as many people as the whole state of Utah.

It's sort of a funny name—where'd it come from?

The Ute Indians. But when most people think of Utah, they think of the Mormons; as many as three-quarters of the population here is Mormon.

Isn't that a religion?

Yes. You sometimes hear it referred to as the Church of Jesus Christ of Latter-Day Saints. They are followers of a man named Joseph Smith Jr. and later, Brigham Young. Utah is the only state where religion plays such a major part in its culture.

Is there really a salt lake around here?

Are you kidding? The Great Salt Lake is the largest one in the whole Western Hemisphere. The size of it changes all the time, depending on the amount of rainfall. It has been as large as 3,000

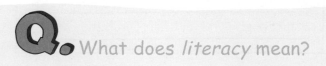

Q. What does *literacy* mean?

square miles, and less than 1,000 square miles during a drought. And because the water has so much salt in it, it makes it really easy to float!

I love the snow! It looks like there's a ton here.

You're not kidding. Up in some of the mountains, it can snow as much as 500 inches a year.

No way! Can we go skiing?

Sure! Sports are so huge in Utah that the 1992 Winter Olympics were here, in Park City. Tourism is a big part of the state's economy. Park City is a great place to ski, and so is Alta. A cool thing about Alta is that they put in their first ski lift in 1939, and then during World War II paratroopers from the Tenth Mountain Regiment came and trained for combat right here on the slopes.

That's a pretty great way to be in the army.

 It refers to people's ability to read. Utah has the highest literacy rate in the nation, at nearly 95 percent!

I've read that a lot of tourists come to Utah for the National Parks, too.

Right again. Bryce Canyon is one of my favorites. Look at this rock here: it has what's called petroglyphs written on it. That's ancient writing from thousand of years ago, from the Native Americans. We can also go to Arches National Park, which has this incredible rock formation called the Delicate Arch.

Holy moley! I've seen that on Utah license plates. I think I remember something else about Utah, though, Laura. Is this where the Transcontinental Railroad was finished?

Good memory, Peter. In 1869, two railroad lines, the Central Pacific and the Union Pacific, met at a place called Promontory Point. The engines from both lines met almost nose to nose, and Central Pacific president Leland Stanford drove in the last spike, which was made of gold!

Wow! There's a souvenir I'd like to bring home from Utah.

Q. Isn't there something odd about the city of Utah named Levan?

A. I'll say! It's "navel" spelled backward, and legend says it was named that because it's smack in the middle of the state.

The state of Vermont was inhabited by the Iroquois and Abenaki Native Americans when Samuel de Champlain claimed it for France in 1609. The French lost the land to the British in 1763 in the French and Indian War.

In 1846, the first United States postage stamp was printed in Brattleboro, Vermont.

State Capital:	Montpelier
Entered the Union:	March 4, 1791—America's fourteenth state, and the first admitted after the Constitution
Largest City:	Burlington
Border States:	Massachusetts, New Hampshire, New York
Land Area:	9,249 square miles
State Bird:	hermit thrush
State Flower:	red clover
State Tree:	sugar maple
State Insect:	honeybee
State Nickname:	the Green Mountain State
State Motto:	"Freedom and Unity"

Brrrr! It's chilly up here!

All the better to ski!

I've never been skiing. Can you teach me?

Oh, sure—I'll take you skating, too.

Wow, all the mountains are so beautiful;
I love New England.

Those are the Green Mountains; believe it or not,
77 percent of Vermont is covered by forest. And don't look
for the ocean—it's the only New England state that doesn't
have a coastline.

Hmmph. Guess that leaves out a trip to the beach.

Not at all! We'll check out Lake Champlain—it's gigantic, and people do all sorts of sports there, just like at an ocean beach. And it has something special: Champy, the monster of the deep!

I've heard of him! He's not real . . . is he?

You'll have to decide for yourself—
more than three hundred
people have reported
seeing him. The sheriff
was the first, back in 1883.

Q. What Vermont blacksmith and inventor said, "I will never put my name on a product that does not have in it the best that is in me."?

Let's think about something less scary, like ice cream. Isn't Ben & Jerry's in Vermont? Let's go get some samples!

We'll need to go to Burlington, which is the largest city in the state, although Montpelier is the capital—the least-populated one in the whole country. In fact, only the state of Wyoming has fewer residents than Vermont.

With so few people, did anyone famous live here—besides Ben and Jerry, that is?

Vermont is the home of two United States presidents: Chester A. Arthur, who was an early believer in civil rights, and Calvin Coolidge, who spoke so little everyone called him "Silent Cal." He's the only president born on July 4, although you may know that presidents John Adams and Thomas Jefferson both died on the *same* Independence Day: America's fiftieth birthday, in 1826.

Do Vermont's Green Mountains have anything to do with Ethan Allen and the Green Mountain Boys?

You've been studying! Ethan Allen led several hundred armed men. They helped Vermonters keep their freedom before the Revolutionary War and then fought together against the British during that War.

Vermonters really know how to tough it out. One guy from Burlington named Horatio Nelson Jackson drove his car across the country on a fifty-dollar bet in 1903. Not only was it a long way, but there weren't any paved roads anywhere outside of the cities.

A. John Deere, inventor in 1837 of the first successful steel plow, and founder of what is now the largest agricultural manufacturing company in the world.

Wow: that's some road trip! Did he stop at that weird little house over the river?

That's not a house, silly—it's a covered bridge. There are more than one hundred of them here. And if you think they were built so people could get out of the rain with their horses, you'd be wrong. The roof and sides are to protect the bridge itself from rotting in the weather. There's even a Covered Bridge Museum!

Leo, why is this candy shaped like a leaf? I've never seen something like that before—mmm, it's delicious, too.

It's maple candy, made from Vermont's own maple syrup. In the late winter and early spring, people tap maple trees and a sap comes out that's made into our famous syrup: the candy's delicious, but the syrup's used mostly for covering waffles and pancakes!

And I happen to know one thing that covers the rough terrain of Vermont: its quarries.

That's right. There are loads of marble and granite quarries here. We tend to think of that stone being used in cemeteries, but these days, people use it to build fancy kitchens, too. And what do people serve in these fancy kitchens: Vermont cheese!

Of course! I've got to take some home to my mom.

Q. Who was Alexander Twilight?

A. He was a Vermonter who was not only the first African American to graduate from an American college, right here at Middlebury College, but also went on to become the first black man elected to the legislature in 1836.

Virginia was the 10th state to join the Union on June 25, 1788. It is the birthplace of eight American presidents: George Washington, Thomas Jefferson, James Madison, James Monroe, William Henry Harrison, John Tyler, Zachary Taylor, and Woodrow Wilson.

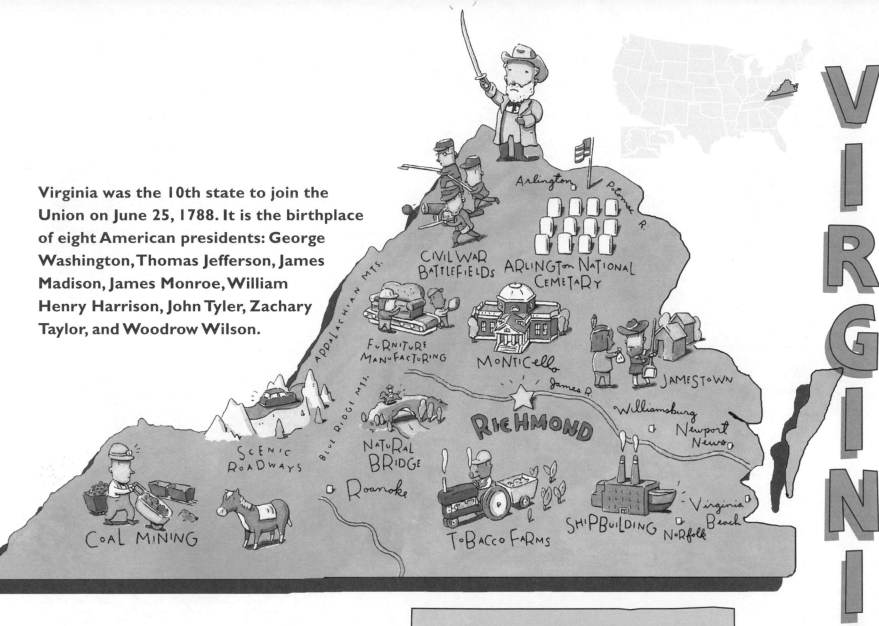

VIRGINIA

State Capital:	Richmond
State Flower:	American dogwood
State Bird:	cardinal
State Dog:	American foxhound
State Shell:	eastern oyster
State Boat:	Chesapeake Bay Deadrise
State Nickname:	Old Dominion
State Motto:	"Sic Semper Tyrannis" ("Thus always to tyrants")
State Slogan:	"Virginia Is for Lovers"

Our trip starts in Jamestown, Penny, site of the first permanent British settlement in North America. Jamestown is on the James River, in the eastern part of Virginia called the Tidewater. Some of it is very beautiful, with wide beaches and the Atlantic Ocean. Many are covered with swamps; the biggest is the Great Dismal Swamp.

A dismal swamp doesn't sound so great to me.

Ha! The first settlers called it Dismal because there were so many snakes they couldn't build anything there!

Washington, D.C., is near Virginia, right, Beau?

Right next door. Virginia donated land to make our capital city. George Washington played such an important role in starting the United States that he's known as "the Father of His Country," so Washington, D.C., is named after him. His leadership as a general during the American Revolution kept the army together.

Q. What is the Piedmont Plateau?

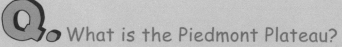

Still, when I think of famous Virginians, I think of Thomas Jefferson.

Me, too. Let's visit Monticello, Thomas Jefferson's home. He spent forty years designing, building, and refining Monticello. The twenty-one-room mansion and plantation is considered one of the most beautiful properties in the United States. Jefferson's telescope is even still here, plus his seven-thousand-book library. He was so interested in education and learning that he even founded and designed the University of Virginia!

Robert E. Lee was a Virginian, too, wasn't he?

He sure was. General Lee led the Confederacy during the Civil War; he was beloved by Southerners and respected by the entire nation. In fact, he was offered the position of head of the Union Army, but turned it down to lead the South and his state, even though he opposed slavery. He was one of this country's toughest soldiers, but when he ordered his men into battle, they refused to let him on the front line, for fear of his being killed.

A.
It is a patchwork of farms where Virginia's most important crops are grown, such as tobacco, wheat, corn, and soybeans. Virginia is also known for raising beef, turkey, and chickens.

Wasn't Richmond the capital of the Confederacy during the Civil War?

Yes, and now of course it's the capital of Virginia. From 1861 to 1865, the armies fought some of the fiercest battles here, trying to capture each other's capital city. More battles were fought in Virginia than in any other state. In some battles, more Americans were killed in a single day than in the entire American Revolution. Today, many of the battlefields are national parks, like Manassas National Battlefield Park. It's so beautiful and peaceful here now that it's hard to imagine thousands of men killing each other here.

That's for sure. I'd like to stop at Arlington National Cemetery. My grandfather is buried there—he fought in Vietnam.

Arlington is the final resting place of 200,000 American soldiers, heroes, and public figures. Row after row of plain, white headstones mark the graves of men and women who fought and died for our country. The Tomb of the Unknown Soldier is here, and the eternal flame where President John F. Kennedy is buried. I think it's the perfect way to say good-bye to Virginia, Penny.

Q. Who is Natty B.?

A. It's not *who*, but *what*! It stands for "natural bridge," and it's the name the locals give to a geological formation in—where else?—Rockbridge County! It's twenty stories high!

Washington became the 42nd state in the Union on November 11, 1889. Washington is the only state named after a United States president (George, of course!)

The popular games Pictionary, Pickle-Ball, and Cranium were all invented in Washington.

State Marine Mammal:	orca
State Amphibian:	Pacific chorus frog
State Tree:	western hemlock
State Vegetable:	Walla Walla sweet onion
State Nickname:	Evergreen State
State Motto:	"Alki" (by and by)
State Song:	"Washington, My Home"
State Folk Song:	"Roll On Columbia, Roll On"

State Capital:	Olympia
State Bird:	willow goldfinch
State Fish:	steelhead trout
State Flower:	coast rhododendron
State Fruit:	apple
State Gem:	petrified wood
State Insect:	green darner dragonfly

WASHINGTON

Look at all these mountains, George—they're covered in snow and it's not even winter.

You're looking at the Olympic Mountains, Mimi; that's how our capital city got its name. Of course, before the settlers came, Native Americans had lived in this territory for thousands of years. They even spoke a language of their own, Lushootseed.

Lushootseed? I can't even say the *name* of the language.

I know. But it was really helpful, because all these different tribes—the Squaxn, Nisqually, Puyallup, Chehalis, Suquamish, and Duwamish—could communicate by speaking the same tongue. In 1792, Europeans came to this part of the country, when Peter Puget and his expedition started mapping the surrounding land. Our whole state is very young compared with much of the country. Believe it or not, the state capitol building in Olympia was a log cabin until 1903!

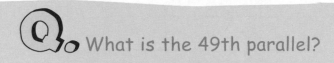 What is the 49th parallel?

Hey, I thought you said you'd take me to a park.

This is a park—Mount Rainer State Park. You're looking at Mount Rainier right now. At 14,410 feet, it's the tallest peak in the Cascade Volcanic Arc. It also has the most glaciers: twenty-six. One of them is called the Nisqually, and it's the fastest-moving glacier in the country—it moves 16 inches a day during the summer! Believe it or not, more than ten thousand people climb Mount Rainier each year. It's really hard to do, and takes two or three days. And no wonder—the National Park Service says that Paradise, an area on the south side of Mount Rainier, is the snowiest place ever measured in the world.

PARADISE
SNOWIEST
PLACE on EARTH

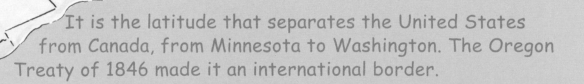

A. It is the latitude that separates the United States from Canada, from Minnesota to Washington. The Oregon Treaty of 1846 made it an international border.

217

Paradise is also the most popular place in the entire park, partly because of the old Paradise Inn, where lots of hikers like to stay. There's also a tree house that's 50 feet up in a red cedar tree, and you can stay overnight!

George, doesn't Bigfoot lurk around here?

Not everyone believes in him, but I totally do! In Canada, they call him Sasquatch, which is Native American for "hairy giant." In Tibet, they call him Yeti—or you might have heard him called the Abominable Snowman, too.

Different tribes all over Washington have sworn for hundreds of years they've seen Bigfoot. He's supposed to have feet as big as a person's size 28 shoe, weigh maybe 900 pounds, and measure 8 feet tall. Some folks say he has only four toes! Lots of scientists say there's no Bigfoot because they've never found old bones. They think people just pull pranks. Not me!

Riding those ferries looks like lots of fun.

Can you believe that Seattle has the biggest fleet of ferries in the country? There were lots of boats here even one hundred years ago, when they were called

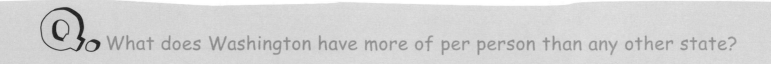

Q. What does Washington have more of per person than any other state?

"the Mosquito Fleet" and were made up of little steamers carrying travelers all over Puget Sound. There are nearly thirty ferries now—some can carry two thousand passengers and more than two hundred cars. They travel all around Seattle, to the San Juan Islands and into Canada.

I see so many people reading: on the ferries, in the parks and coffeehouses—everywhere!

It's funny you noticed. Seattle not only has more college graduates than any other city in the United States, it's also the most literate city.

I guess it's time to say "Alki," huh, George?

You're right, Mimi. It's the state motto and is Chinook for "by and by," as in, "I'll be seeing you by and by."

A. Coffee bean roasters! Washington is considered the coffee capital of the United States. (Starbucks started in Seattle!)

WEST VIRGINIA

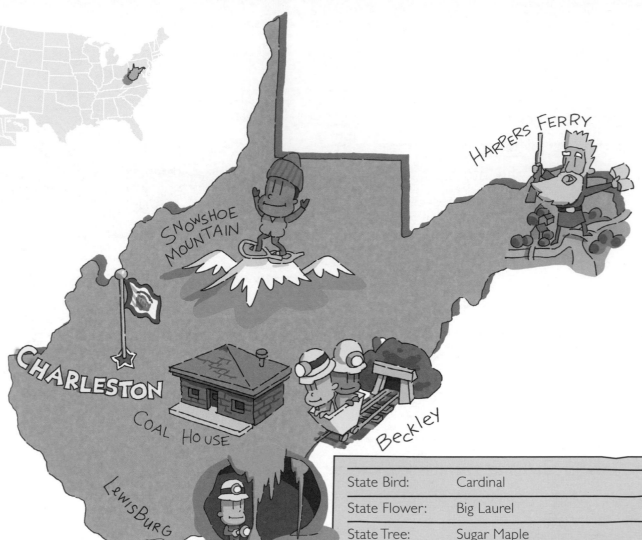

SNOWSHOE MOUNTAIN

HARPERS FERRY

CHARLESTON

COAL HOUSE

Beckley

LewisBurg

West Virginia became a state on June 20, 1863. It was an important border state between the North and South in the Civil War.

Q. What's the capital of West Virginia?

State Bird:	Cardinal
State Flower:	Big Laurel
State Tree:	Sugar Maple
State Animal:	Black Bear
State Butterfly:	Monarch Butterfly
State Day:	West Virginia Day, June 20
State Fish:	Brook Trout
State Fruit:	Apple, Golden Delicious Apple
State Gem:	Chalcedony
State Reptile:	Timber rattlesnake
State Nickname:	Mountain State
State Motto:	"Montani semper liberi" ("Mountaineers are always free")
State Songs:	"West Virginia, My Home Sweet Home," "The West Virginia Hills," "This is My West Virginia"

West Virginia is in a funny spot geographically. It's called the southernmost northern state, and the northernmost southern state.

That's sort of nutty, Carri. Why?

Partly it has to do with this imaginary border called the Mason-Dixon Line, which divided some of the British colonies back in the 1760s, before there was even a United States. Later it became a line people used to divide the Northern and Southern states in America.

But how did this affect West Virginia?

Well, Leo, West Virginia is along the Mason-Dixon Line now, but before the Civil War it was part of Virginia. There *was* no West Virginia until it seceded from Virginia during the war. The citizens in that part of Virginia felt more like Northerners in the Civil War; for example, they were against slavery. So they left Virginia and formed their own state. See what I mean? The southernmost northern state!

Or, the northernmost southern state! Yeah, I get it now.

But before all that, there were Native Americans where West Virginia is now. Let's go check out Moundville and you'll see.

A. It's been Charleston since 1885, but it was moved so often it was called the "floating capital." This is the second time it's been Charleston—it was Wheeling twice, too!

Holy cow! What is that gigantic hill?

It's the biggest Indian burial ground in America; it's been here about two thousand years. And this is the craziest part: historians think that these people, called the Adena, didn't use horses or even anything with a wheel when building. They just carried all the dirt in baskets. Amazing, considering it's over 60 feet high and 240 feet around!

Gee, it sure is hilly here.

Funny you should say that: West Virginia's nickname is "the Mountain State," and its motto is "Mountaineers Are Always Free." There are tunnels and bridges everywhere because of the terrain. The New River Gorge Bridge is my favorite. It's a steel-arch bridge more than a half mile long. They have an annual Bridge Day, where people parachute off and rappel, which is like mountain climbing. It's mad cool!

Cool? Yikes, it sounds scary.

Ha! Then I'll bet you wouldn't want to meet the black bear, West Virginia's state animal.

No. I would not!

Q. Who is John Henry?

Maybe fishing is more your speed then. All kinds of fishing are big here, because of course lots of mountains means lots of rivers. Trout fishing is my favorite.

Sounds like fun! Hey, what's with that weird black house over there?

It's made entirely of coal—69 tons of it! Coal mining is one of West Virginia's biggest businesses, so someone built it back in 1933 as a publicity stunt. Logging is also important. Nearly 75 percent of the state is covered by forest. People work really hard here. Maybe that's why the very first spa was opened here in Berkeley Springs.

Yeah, but this sign says it opened in 1756. I'll bet it wasn't very fancy—they didn't even have electricity then!

The Native Americans came here and relaxed in the warm mineral waters. The town is even called Bath! But maybe the most important thing about West Virginia is that the entire state is a part of the United States called Appalachia. Parts of Appalachia are very poor, but there's a rich tradition of music, crafts, and much more. And it's so beautiful!

A. He's an African-American folk hero also called the "steel-drivin' man." Known as the strongest man alive, legend has it that he was faster than a steam hammer!

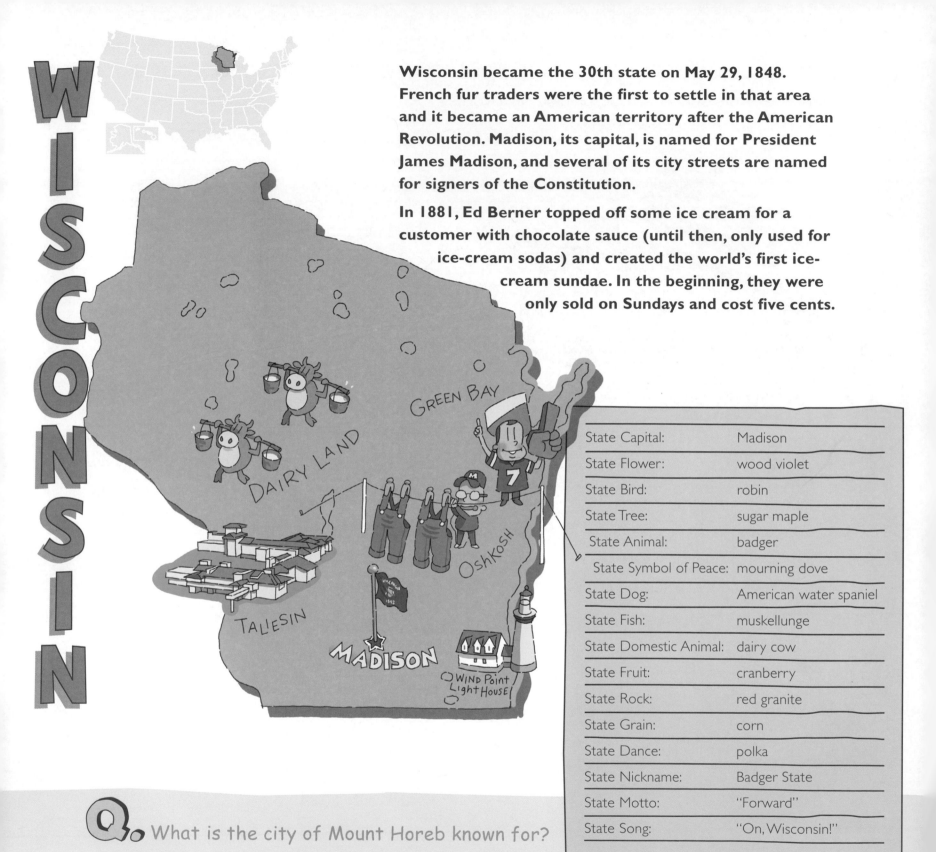

WISCONSIN

Wisconsin became the 30th state on May 29, 1848. French fur traders were the first to settle in that area and it became an American territory after the American Revolution. Madison, its capital, is named for President James Madison, and several of its city streets are named for signers of the Constitution.

In 1881, Ed Berner topped off some ice cream for a customer with chocolate sauce (until then, only used for ice-cream sodas) and created the world's first ice-cream sundae. In the beginning, they were only sold on Sundays and cost five cents.

Q. What is the city of Mount Horeb known for?

State Capital:	Madison
State Flower:	wood violet
State Bird:	robin
State Tree:	sugar maple
State Animal:	badger
State Symbol of Peace:	mourning dove
State Dog:	American water spaniel
State Fish:	muskellunge
State Domestic Animal:	dairy cow
State Fruit:	cranberry
State Rock:	red granite
State Grain:	corn
State Dance:	polka
State Nickname:	Badger State
State Motto:	"Forward"
State Song:	"On, Wisconsin!"

Mooooooo!

Ha! I get the joke, George. Here we are in Wisconsin, "the Dairy Capital of the World." We get more milk, cheese, and butter from this state than from any other in the country.

Wait, you know about the Cheeseheads, right?

Who?

It used to be that sports fans from Illinois made fun of Wisconsinites, calling them "Cheeseheads." But then a Wisconsin man made a hat shaped like a wedge of Swiss cheese and everyone from Wisconsin loved it. Now they call *themselves* Cheeseheads.

That's why you see all those hats at the Green Bay Packers games! I love them.

Something else is cool about the Green Bay Packers: the team is owned by the fans. More than 100,000 people have bought stock in the Packers. When you watch games on TV, you can really feel the hometown love.

A. It calls itself "Troll Capital of the World"; they are featured on people's lawns, even on the street signs! Local folklore says they protect the crops.

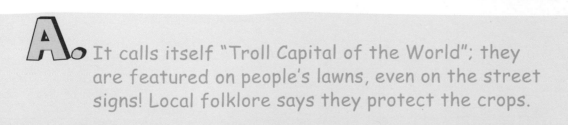

That is so awesome! Without cheese, milk, and butter, there'd be no ice cream, no buttered popcorn, no milk-shakes. Life wouldn't be worth living.

I agree. It would be great to grow up in Wisconsin. Some famous people came from this state, like Harry Houdini, Frank Lloyd Wright, and Barbara Millicent Roberts.

I know who Houdini is, because I love magic tricks. Who are the other two?

Frank Lloyd Wright is one of the greatest architects ever. More than one hundred years ago he began designing houses that blended in with nature and were part of their surroundings. He would even design the furniture for his houses! This is way before people were thinking about ecology.

And Barbara Millicent Roberts? She sounds familiar.

She ought to—that's Barbie's real name! She was "born" here in Wisconsin in 1959.

Really? I heard she and Ken broke up, but are back together again.

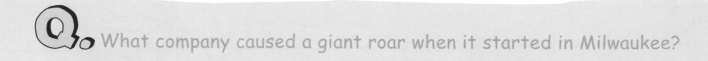

Q. What company caused a giant roar when it started in Milwaukee?

Let's go to the town of Cable and see the start of the big race.

What race?

You'll love it: it's the American Birkebeiner—people call it "the Birkie"—a 50-kilometer cross-country ski race, the largest of its kind in the world. There's also a Junior Birkie, too, for kids. Even some Olympic athletes come!

As long as there's some hot chocolate at the other end, I'm in! What do you suppose is the big event in Wisconsin in the summer?

Milwaukee, Wisconsin's biggest city, hosts Summerfest every year. It's a gigantic music festival, so big that Guinness World Records says it's the largest in the whole world. Sometimes people call it "the Big Gig," and you can see why. More than seven hundred bands perform, playing everything: folk, gospel, rock, hip-hop, jazz—you name it!

Awesome! How long does it go on?

Eleven whole days.

Let's go—I just want to make sure we have time to go to Noah's Ark.

A. Harley-Davidson. They've been making heavyweight motorcycles since 1903. Co-founder Arthur Davidson said he wanted to invent something that would "take the hard work out of pedaling a bicycle."

Noah's Ark? From the Bible?

Don't tell me you don't know Noah's Ark. Of course it's named after the Bible, but it's the biggest water park in the entire USA!

No way! The longest water coaster—Black Anaconda. Scary! The sign says there are forty-nine water slides. I must be in heaven!

You know, speaking of scary, you know what Wisconsin's first inhabitants did? Well, actually, it was about 10,000 BC, so it wasn't Wisconsin yet. They were Paleo-Indians and they hunted mastodons and mammoths!

That is *way* scary. When did explorers come—and from where?

In 1634, Frenchman Jean Nicolet came through what is now Wisconsin. Believe it or not, he was looking for a water route to China by going through North America!

Imagine if he had run across Noah's Ark!

Wyoming was the 44th state to join the Union on July 10, 1890. Its shape is called a geoellipsoidal rectangle.

State Bird:	Meadowlark
State Flower:	Indian Paintbrush
State Tree:	Plains Cottonwood
State Mammal:	Bison
State Butterfly:	Sheridan's green hairstreak butterfly
State Reptile:	Horned Toad
State Fish:	Cutthroat Trout
State Dinosaur:	Triceratops
State Coin:	Sacajawea golden dollar coin
State Sport:	Rodeo
State Gemstone:	Jade
State Nickname:	Equality State
State Motto:	"Equal Rights"
State Song:	"Wyoming"

I can tell you right away what my favorite thing is about Wyoming.

The mountains? The wide open spaces? The skiing?

Nope. What I love is that before Wyoming was even a state, when it was a territory back in 1869, it gave women the right to vote.

Go, Wyoming! It's probably as beautiful here now as it ever was. There aren't many people here building big cities; Cheyenne, the capital, is the largest. It has the fewest residents of any of the fifty states; less than 600,000, which is usually the population of a medium-size city.

Maybe the *other* very best thing about Wyoming is that it's home to most of Yellowstone National Park. When the United States made it a national park in 1872, not only was it the first one in our country, but the first national park in the whole world.

Oh, wait, I'll bet you don't know about these two explorers: John Colter was a guy with the Lewis and Clark Expedition, and he wrote about the area that's now Yellowstone in 1807. So did another man named Jim Bridger, a trapper and trailblazer. When they described how beautiful it was around Yellowstone, everyone who read about it said they were making it all up—it sounded too good to be true!

Q. What was America's first national monument?

Well, let's go! I've always wanted to take a trip there and see Old Faithful. Thar she blows!

Yup, every hour!

Rick, do you think we'll see jackelopes at Yellowstone?

Carla, jackelopes aren't real! A Wyoming man name Douglas Herrick made them up. He said they were a combination of a pygmy deer and a killer rabbit.

Yeah, well I'll believe it when I *don't* see it!

OK, here's a weird thing about Wyoming. You know the Rocky Mountains

are here, but you might not know about the Continental Divide. It runs from north to south through the United States, and separates the watersheds, so that everything drains either to the west to the Pacific Ocean, or to the east, eventually to the Atlantic or the Gulf of Mexico.

Gee, that's some long trip for a snow-flake or drop of rain to make.

No kidding. You know, Wyoming does more coal mining than any other state. The Powder River basin, where a lot of it comes from, is formed by the runoff to the west of the Continental Divide. It's one of the state's biggest businesses.

A. Devils Tower, named in 1906, is a volcanic rock formation in Wyoming's Black Hills. People remember it as the mountain where the spaceship landed in the movie *Close Encounters of the Third Kind.*

I heard dude ranches were invented here.

You're right! The Bar B C Ranch was built back in 1912 to cater to guests who were beginning to hear so much about "the West" and Yellowstone and were curious to check it all out. People didn't really want to "rough it"—just pretend they were as tough as cowboys. The ranch owner called the guests "dudes," and that's where the word came from.

Dude! You're kidding!

Very funny. I'll tell you about two guys in these parts who weren't dudes, though: Butch Cassidy and the Sundance Kid.

I love that movie!

In real life they were pretty tough bank robbers. Their real names were Robert LeRoy Parker and Harry Longabaugh, and they terrorized folks all over Wyoming. In fact, Hole in the Wall, a notorious outlaw hideout, was located near Butch's ranch.

Say, where does the name "Wyoming" come from, anyway?

It's a word from the Delaware Indians, meaning "mountains and valleys alternating."

That's a pretty good name, except it could never describe how pretty it is.

Q. Why is it that Wyoming is an almost perfect rectangle?

A. It's one of only three states, with Utah and Colorado, that has borders defined by latitude and longitude, not natural geographic boundaries.

J.P. you're not trying to trick me, are you? I *know* Washington DC is a city, not a state.

No, Lorraine, but it's so important, it feels a little like our fifty-first state. Our entire country is run from here, after all, even though it's smaller than any state in the union.

Our forefathers wrote in the Constitution that there should be a separate district, connected in no way to another state.

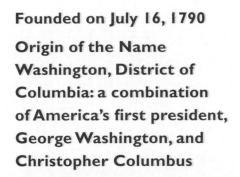

So George Washington hired a Frenchman named Pierre Charles L'Enfant to make a plan for a city that all American citizens could enjoy.

An important part is called the National Mall, and it's not at all a mall like we think of today. It's a beautiful outdoor park, with the United States Capitol at one end and the famous Washington Monument at the other.

Founded on July 16, 1790

Origin of the Name Washington, District of Columbia: a combination of America's first president, George Washington, and Christopher Columbus

Major Industry:	government
Official Bird:	wood thrush
Official Tree:	scarlet oak
Official Flower:	American Beauty rose
Official Motto:	"Justia Omnibus" (Justice for All)
Official Song:	"The Star-Spangled Banner"

Nearby is the White House at 1600 Pennsylvania Avenue. It's huge!

I've read that it has 132 rooms—what a great place to play hide-and-seek! There are thirty-five bathrooms, a bowling alley, and a movie theater. It's six stories high, including two basements, and it contains secret passageways, some people say. It was the first government building in Washington.

FIRE! 1812

ADDITIONS 1906

Redecorate 1960

stuff

Did you know it was burned down by the British in the War of 1812? It was new then: John Adams was the first president to live there in 1800. It's been changed lots since then. The West Wing was built to add office space, and by 1949, the White House was in such bad shape that they took the entire insides out and rebuilt it. Then in the 1960s, there was a historic restoration. Who knows what will happen next? Still, it will always belong to every American.

Q. What right did Washingtonians not have until 1961 that every other American had?

Y ou know, Lorraine, there are the fifty United States, but there are also other places —all islands— that are considered territories.

What? I don't get it.

Well, you might not hear too much about them. There are several islands or island groups way out in the Pacific Ocean that the U.S. government helps oversee. Many of them were oc-cupied by the Japanese during World War II, because they are situated between California and Japan. Several of these territories—American Samoa, Palau, the Federated States of Micronesia, Guam, the Marshall Islands, and the North Mariana Islands—have a representative in Congress, but their inhabitants are not U.S. citizens.

So we're sort of like caretakers.

That's right. Now the two you hear most about, Puerto Rico and the U.S. Virgin Islands, are a little different. Their people are U.S. citizens, but they do not have the right to vote.

It's confusing! Will any of these territories ever become one of our United States?

I guess we'll have to wait and see—from what we've seen of how the first came to be fifty, it looks like anything can happen!

A. The right to vote in a federal election! Because it was technically not a state, these citizens who lived in the same city as the president weren't even allowed to vote for him!

U.S. POSSESSIONS

You all sure do know your stuff. We were talking when you all first arrived about our flag, and how it's changed over the years. Since you're here on July 4, Independence Day, I think I can promise that you're going to see an American flag like none you've ever seen before.

Hey, look everybody—fireworks!

And that one's shaped like a flag! Happy Fourth of July, United States—all fifty of them!